Build Your
Own Network
Sales Business

Build Your Own Network Sales Business

Gregory Kishel

Patricia Kishel

John Wiley & Sons, Inc.

New York · Chichester · Brisbane · Toronto · Singapore

In recognition of the importance of preserving what has been written, it is a policy of John Wiley & Sons, Inc., to have books of enduring value published in the United States printed on acid-free paper, and we exert our best efforts to that end.

Library of Congress Cataloging-in-Publication Data:

Kishel, Gregory F., 1946–
    Build your own network sales business / Gregory Kishel, Patricia Kishel.

      p.   cm.
    Includes bibliographical references.
    ISBN 0-471-53692-X (alk. paper) — ISBN 0-471-53691-1
(pbk. : alk. paper)
    1. Multilevel marketing   I. Kishel, Patricia Gunter, 1948–
II. Title.
HF5415.126K57   1991   91-193408
658.8'43—dc20

Printed in the United States of America

10 9 8 7 6 5 4 3 2 1

Printed and bound by the Courier Companies, Inc.

Contents

Build Your Own Network Sales Business

1

Multilevel Marketing—The Power of Many

Multilevel marketing (MLM)—using "people power," rather than conventional advertising and retail institutions, to promote and sell a company's goods and services—is fast becoming one of the leading marketing methods of the decade. In addition to benefiting the companies that use it, multilevel marketing (or "network marketing," as it is often called) is providing an opportunity for individuals to earn sizeable incomes as independent distributors.

Just as franchising opened the door on entrepreneurship for millions of prospective businessowners in the 1970s and 1980s, MLM (multilevel marketing) is now doing the same thing—at a fraction of the start-up cost.

WHAT IS MULTILEVEL MARKETING?

Multilevel marketing is a method of selling in which customers have the option of becoming product distributors, who in turn develop "downlines," or levels of distributors beneath them, all levels sharing in the profits of the level(s) below them. Bypassing traditional wholesaler-retailer arrangements and expensive advertising media, MLM companies, in effect, rely on networks of independent distributors to reach customers by word of mouth. Money that would otherwise go to middlemen and promotion specialists goes to network members instead, resulting in savings for the MLM companies and earnings for the distributor-entrepreneurs.

Although the basic MLM structure has been successfully employed by MLM giants such as Amway and Shaklee since the late 1950s, the MLM industry itself is still considered to be in its infancy. This is due to both the number of new companies (many of them major corporations) that are choosing to use MLM and also the growing interest of managers and professionals in becoming distributors. Network marketing was once thought to apply only to the selling of personal care and household products; that is no longer the case. Now the product being sold is just as likely to be a computer program, financial advice, a travel package, or a book, sold by one business executive to another.

HOW MLM WORKS

The MLM concept is a simple one. Essentially it is a nonstorefront way of selling products and services through a tiered structure of independent distributors. A company that decides to use this marketing method starts by making its product offering available to a small number of highly motivated people in key sales regions. In exchange for selling the company's merchandise and signing up new distributors, the initial distributors are given the opportunity to earn sales commissions and to build their own sales organizations, or networks. The new distributors who join the company are given the same opportunities as the initial distributors, and, as the process repeats itself, the MLM company's distribution system expands, spreading from person to person, from state to state, and even, in some cases, from country to country.

For the process to work, the relationship between the MLM company and its distributors must benefit both parties. From the company's point of view, the costs of supporting the distribution network—providing sales brochures, audio and video tapes, holding presentation meetings, warehousing and transporting merchandise— should be less than that of using standard retailing channels. From the distributor's point of view, the start-up costs and working-capital expenditures should be both affordable and reasonable with respect to the profit to be gained. Equally important is the fact that the earnings potential should justify the degree of effort that the business venture requires.

As you can see from the accompanying chart on page 4, network marketing has definite advantages and disadvantages, which companies seeking to employ it and prospective entrepreneurs seeking to become involved in it must carefully evaluate.

When the circumstances are right and the advantages

THE ADVANTAGES AND DISADVANTAGES
OF MULTILEVEL MARKETING

From the Company's Viewpoint

Advantages

- Reduced capital investment
- Reduced advertising expenditures
- Motivated salesforce
- Positive word of mouth
- Increased customer loyalty
- High repeat sales

Disadvantages

- Longer start-up time
- Increased administrative duties
- Less control
- More paperwork
- Need to develop sales training and promotional materials
- Danger that company's image can be harmed by overzealous members

From the Distributor's Viewpoint

Advantages

- High earnings potential
- Low initial investment, usually under $150.00
- Be your own boss
- Operating the business from home
- Buying a product you like at the wholesale price
- Tax advantages
- No franchise fees to pay
- Opportunity to make new friends
- Possible involvement of family members

Disadvantages

- Long hours
- Demands on your time by network members
- Difficulty in selling product
- MLM guidelines to follow
- Actions of other MLM members reflect on you
- Selling expenses
- Staying motivated
- Possible minimum inventory purchases
- Necessity of staying active in company so as not to lose network.

outweigh the disadvantages for both the company and the distributor, then network marketing is an option to be considered.

MONEY—THE MULTIPLIER EFFECT

Now that you have an idea of how MLM works and have studied the advantages and disadvantages, you may be thinking, This is all very well and good, but can I get **rich** in MLM?

That depends on the company and on you.

The amount of money you can earn in MLM is directly related to your ability to sell the product or service you represent and to recruit others to sell the product, as well. In the beginning, your business would look this:

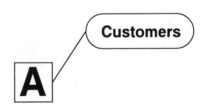

The money you (A) make at this level would be computed by multiplying your sales commission rate by your total sales volume. Thus, if your commission rate were 50 percent of the product's retail price, on sales of $1,000, you would receive $500.

Part of the beauty of MLM, though, is its "Multiplier Effect," or the ability to make money not only from your own sales, but from those of the people you bring into the organization and from those of the people they bring in. For example, if you were to bring in three other people, who, in turn, bring in three additional people, your business would look like this:

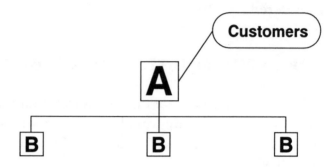

and then like this:

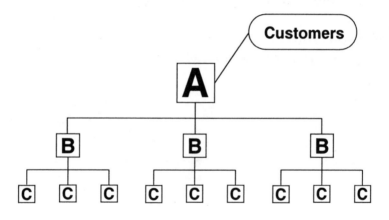

You would continue to earn a 50 percent commission on all the merchandise that you personally sell *plus* a percentage of the sales generated by each of the twelve network members. Depending on the terms of your MLM company, the average amount of that percentage would typically be 5 to 20 percent. So, if your twelve distributors sell a total of $12,000 worth of merchandise, at a 10 percent commission rate, you would receive an additional $1,200.

Each MLM organization has its own marketing plan that outlines how many levels a distributor can have beneath him or her and the percentage payouts at the various levels. One MLM organization may allow a distributor to have five levels, while another may allow seven or more. Generally, the percentage of sales rate goes up, too, as you increase the number of levels in your network. So, if your network is three levels deep, you would receive a higher average percentage of network members' sales than someone whose network has only two levels.

To really reap the rewards of network marketing, your goal should be to build your MLM network to three levels and to have each of the people you sponsor do the same.

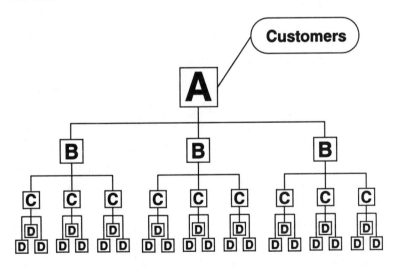

Once you have built three levels into your MLM network and you have a solid organizational base, you can work with the members below you to help them build their groups, too.

WAYS TO GENERATE INCOME

There are a number of different types of compensation plans utilized by MLM companies. Some of the most common elements of these plans include:

- *Commissions on Personal Sales.* This is what you make on the goods *you* actually sell. It is the difference between the wholesale price of goods (the price you pay as a distributor for goods to deliver to customers) and the selling price (what the customer pays to buy the goods from you).
- *Group Bonus.* Also known as an "override," this is the percentage you receive of the dollar sales volume generated by the members in your network.
- *Leadership Bonus.* This is a bonus with which many organizations reward network members whenever they help someone they have sponsored move up to a higher level in the organization.
- *Residual Income.* This is an opportunity that network marketers often have to earn residual income on customers' repurchases or renewals of products or services, just as songwriters and TV actors earn royalties year after year on earlier work. Thus, when this compensation method is offered, even if you do not personally make the sale the next time, you still receive a commission for it.
- *Usage Bonus.* This bonus, offered by many MLM companies that provide membership services such as discounts on air travel, and telephone and credit card charges, is paid to distributors as a percentage of their groups' total purchase, or usage, levels.

Given their emphasis on people power to market their wares, MLM companies do, indeed, offer network members a wide variety of compensation methods beyond the ordinary. Unlike the "linear" incomes most people make—a day's pay for a day's work—MLM offers the possibility of "multiplex" income, that is, earnings from several sources over an extended period of time.

The potential to accumulate great wealth is certainly present in those MLM companies that have solid marketing plans and that provide customers with desirable products and services. In many instances, new recruits to network marketing have begun earning monthly incomes in the five-figure range within a year of joining their companies. And success stories about self-made MLM millionaires abound in the network marketing industry. As MLM members themselves are quick to point out, though, a key part of the word *network* is *work*. Even with the best MLM companies, in order to achieve any degree of financial success, you have to be prepared to put in the necessary time and energy to make your network grow.

2

Choosing the Right Opportunity

Once you have made up your mind to become involved in network marketing, the next most important decision to make is which MLM company to join. Here it is vital that you research each company under consideration to find out as much as possible about its products, policies, and procedures. <u>Don't make the mistake of signing up to become a distributor on the basis of a friend's recommendation alone.</u> Just because an MLM company is right for one person does not mean it will be right for you. To succeed as a network marketer, you must find a business that meets your own individual needs and will enable you to achieve your specific goals.

Rather than worrying about "missing the boat" on a "hot opportunity," your primary concern should be to find the opportunity that's best for you. That takes time. As for "missing the boat," that isn't going to happen. If an MLM company is really as good as it first appears to be, the opportunity it provides will be just as good a few days, or weeks, later when you're ready to join.

EVALUATING A COMPANY

In evaluating an MLM company, there are several sources of information that you can utilize to get the answers you need. These include:

- *Sales Presentations.*   Attend one or more sales presentations, or "opportunity meetings" as they are frequently called, to hear the company's story and to meet current and prospective network members.
- *Distributors.*   Talk to people who are already in the company and ask them to share their experiences with it. Ask questions about the number of hours they put into the business each week, the financial investment required, the quality of the company's products, the training and support programs, the amount of money they are earning, and so on.
- *Customers.*   Talk to the people who actually buy and use the company's product and find out why they like it, how often they buy it, and how long they have been customers.
- *Promotional Materials.*   Examine the brochures and audio and video tapes used to promote the company and its products. See if they are professional in appearance. Decide, as well as you can, if the claims they make are realistic and truthful.
- *Training Materials.*   Ask about the types of training materials that the company provides to assist you in developing your selling and recruitment skills, for example, a handbook or some kind of "quick start kit" to get you going, or time management and personal motivation tapes.
- *Annual Reports.*   If you really want to get the inside facts on an MLM company, examine its annual re-

ports for the last few years. The information pertaining to its assets and liabilities, revenues and expenses, investments, top management, and board of directors is one of the best indicators you can use to determine the overall reliability and financial soundness of a company.

- *Trade Associations.* Check out the company with the trade associations listed at the back of this book. Ask for information about the company's performance record, number of years in business, company management and whether there have ever been any complaints lodged against it.
- *Government Agencies.* Contact your state Attorney General's office and the Federal Trade Commission to obtain any information they may have on file about the company.
- *The Media.* Find out if there have been any stories about the company in recent magazine or newspaper articles, on radio or television. Note whether the coverage was favorable or critical.
- *Competitors.* Talk to the competition, too. These are the people you will be competing with to make sales and to recruit network members. Make sure that the company you elect to join has a clear advantage over the others in its field.

- *The Company's Products.* Before you decide to become a distributor, make it a point to try out the products you'll be selling to see how you like them. If you're not 100 percent satisfied, you probably should pass on the business opportunity. Unless you believe in the products yourself, you'll have a difficult time convincing others to buy them.

The more information sources you turn to, the better. Once you have the data you need to make your evaluation, you can use it to rate the company in these areas: (1) product offering, (2) strength of the company, (3) industry attractiveness, (4) type of compensation plan, (5) marketing support, and (6) training program.

Product Offering

First and foremost, does the company offer the types of products or services that you would like to sell? If you have no interest in computers or hate to cook, then an MLM company that specializes in computer-related services or sells a line of upscale cookware probably isn't for you—regardless of the earnings potential it may provide.

Along with keeping sight of your own interests, you should also evaluate the product offering in terms of its quality. Does the company maintain high standards of quality control? Does it stand behind the merchandise it sells? What kinds of warranties or refund policies are there? Beware of unsubstantiated claims ("This product will change your life") and hype ("The most revolutionary invention since the wheel"). As a distributor, you would be hard-pressed to deliver on such promises and could be held liable for any false representations that you make to customers.

Having a good product alone isn't enough. The product offering must be competitively priced and in tune with consumers' needs. For example, a high-quality line of woodworking tools could prove to be a tough sell if people were to suddenly decide that plastic is "in" and wood is "out." Thus, part of your evaluation of the product offering should include an assessment of the marketing environment in which the product will be sold. This involves looking at such factors as changing lifestyles (the growth of two-paycheck families, increased interest in nutrition and physical fitness, the desire for more leisure time), new technologies that are being developed, the economy, and the competition.

Does the MLM company offer just one product or service or a "line" of products from which to choose? The advantage of a line is the opportunity it gives distributors to make multiple sales or to offer customers alternative selections if one product isn't right for them.

Most important of all, you should look for a product or service that has a high "repeatability quotient"; that is, it should be something that people use again and again and buy on a repeat basis. This will put you in a good position to develop a loyal following of customers already presold on the product offering.

Strength of the Company

The strength of an MLM company can be measured in many ways—the number of years it has been in business, demonstrated financial success, position within its industry, the quality of its management team, its marketing plan, and so on. In examining these factors, along with any others that you think are important, try to get a sense of the direction in which the company is headed and its ability to consistently deliver the quality products and the leadership advice necessary for you to build a profitable network.

The first three factors—years in business, financial success, and industry position—are all historical in nature. They show what the company has done, but not what it is capable of doing. To *stay* successful, a company must know how to make the best use of its resources and must be able to anticipate and react to change. This is why it's important to pay close attention to the company's management team and overall marketing strategy, as well. What are the professional and educational backgrounds of the top managers in the company? How long have they been involved in network marketing? What new products or services is the company planning to offer? What pricing or promotion changes are being developed? What customer groups are identified as new target markets?

Industry Attractiveness

Does the MLM company operate in an industry that's growing or shrinking? For example, during the 1970s, when the nation's birth rate was low, companies that sold baby-related goods—infant clothes, toys, furniture, and personal-care products—fared badly. During the 1980s, though, when the "Baby Boom" generation started having children, the baby-products industry took off.

In addition to reflecting the times, the industry should be one that is, in general, viewed favorably by the public and in the press. Since network marketing is built around "friends telling friends" about the products or services they represent, it is important for the industry to have a positive image. Otherwise you're likely to end up spending more time defending the company than selling its products.

Type of Compensation Plan

One area of obvious interest to you should be the company's compensation plan. This should be equitable and realistic, rewarding people on the basis of their productivity and on the productivity of their network members. Among the points to consider are:

- The commission rate paid on sales you personally make.
- The bonus percentages, or overrides, paid out on network members' sales at each level.
- The other types of bonuses that can be earned, such as leadership bonuses, usage bonuses, and renewal bonuses.
- The requirements (number of people in your network and/or sales volume) for advancing from one level to the next.
- Number of lower network levels on which you can receive bonuses.
- Minimum monthly sales volume required in order to remain an active distributor.
- How and when commissions and bonuses are to be paid.

Bear in mind that if a plan looks too good to be true, it probably is. A more modest, but attainable, plan is always better than one that makes glowing promises but fails to deliver. Also, the compensation plan should be easy to understand and easy to explain to others. The more complicated a plan is, the greater the chance for errors and misunderstandings to arise.

Marketing Support

Even the most articulate network marketer needs help in describing the benefits of the company's products or services and in explaining the advantages of becoming a distributor. A good MLM company should be able to provide the sales brochures, catalogs, forms, audio and video tapes, and other promotional materials that it takes to conduct successful selling or recruitment sessions. Along with this, the people above you in the organization (your "upline") and the company's corporate staff, as well, should be available to assist you in developing your marketing strategy and in giving presentations to prospective customers and network members.

In evaluating the promotional materials that are provided, look to see that they are both appealing and forthright. It is important that they look professional and show the company and its product offering at their best. At the same time, though, they mustn't use inflated representations or false claims to do so. One rule of thumb to use in assessing promotional materials is to ask yourself if you would feel comfortable using them or giving them out to others. You should also find out what the materials cost and if you will be required to purchase a specific amount of them as part of a standard inventory. Since promotional materials cannot be resold and often cannot be returned to the company for a refund, you want to be careful not to buy more supplies than you need.

Training Program

In addition to providing marketing support, the MLM company should also have a strong training program to assist distributors in developing the sales and management skills it takes to build a solid network. Among the types of training assistance that should be available to you are: a distributor's handbook to answer the day-to-day questions that come up; audio tapes on selling, time management, motivation, and other aspects of running a network marketing business; and video tapes of sales presentations. Most MLM companies also sponsor workshops and seminars throughout the year, and a growing number have gone so far as to establish telephone "hotlines" that distributors can call to get information.

To make sure that you'll have the help you need when you want it, get the full details of the company's program in advance. If a company is unwilling or unable to prepare an adequate training program, this should be viewed as a "red flag." It could be a signal that the company is undercapitalized and can't afford to spend the money on a program. It could also mean that the company lacks professional expertise or simply doesn't care about training. Whatever the reason, the distributors are ultimately left to fend for themselves.

AVOIDING PYRAMID SCHEMES

In choosing an MLM company, make sure that the company you select really *is* a network marketing company and not an illegal pyramid scheme. Since both have the same organizational structure, it is easy to confuse the two. Legitimate MLM companies generate income from sales of a product to consumers; pyramids generate income simply from bringing in new members and charging them fees.

Pyramid schemes (also known as "Ponzi schemes" after the man who originated the concept) operate much like a chain letter with newcomers to the group (or chain) paying money to those already in the group. Once in the pyramid, the only way to make money yourself is to bring in new people who, in turn, pay you a fee. The problem with pyramid schemes, and the reason that they are illegal, is that only the first people who join have a chance of making any money. Eventually the pyramid collapses when the people on the bottom discover that there's no one left to bring into the group.

Some of the more devious pyramid schemes actually do offer a product for sale, but the "product" is nothing more than window dressing. Rather than selling it to consumers at a profit, distributors at one level in the pyramid sell it at a profit to the distributors on the level beneath them. Those distributors do the same. And so the product goes, passing from one level in the pyramid to the next, until finally those distributors on the bottom are left "holding the bag"—stuck with overpriced goods that can't be sold.

Two of the most common tip-offs that a company is an illegal pyramid scheme are (1) using *headhunting fees* and (2) engaging in *inventory loading.* A company that uses headhunting fees pays members for bringing in new recruits who are charged an entry fee to join the organization. A company that engages in inventory loading requires new distributors to purchase large amounts of nonreturnable merchandise. Part of the company's proceeds from each distributor's order then goes to that person's sponsor.

Therefore, to avoid getting involved in a pyramid scheme, watch out for any company that:

- Promises extremely high earnings.
- Downplays the importance of hard work and personal sacrifice in achieving success.
- Is more interested in recruiting new members than in making sales to consumers.
- Pays headhunting fees for new recruits.
- Charges a high entry fee to become a distributor.
- Does not have a product or service to sell.
- Has a product with a low repeatability quotient—people may buy it once, but not on a regular basis.
- Is structured so that only the distributors at the bottom of the organization actually sell to consumers.
- Requires new distributors to purchase large amounts of inventory.
- Has an inadequate "buy back" policy for unsold inventory.

ASSESSING YOUR OWN NEEDS

At the same time you are evaluating MLM companies, you should also look within yourself and ask the question "What do *I* want?" By identifying your own needs and determining what is important to you, you'll be better equipped to choose a business opportunity that will enable you to achieve your goals both personally and professionally.

To assess your needs, start by asking yourself these questions:

1. What type of MLM business would I enjoy running?
2. Which work activities give me the greatest amount of satisfaction?

3. What do I need to accomplish to consider myself a business success?

4. Do I want to get involved in network marketing on a full-time or part-time basis?

5. Is this going to be my primary or secondary source of income?

6. Am I looking for an MLM business that my family can participate in, too?

7. What are my income goals?

8. What kinds of recognition are important to me?

9. Would I rather work with people on a one-to-one basis or in a group?

10. How much of a risk am I willing to take?

The more closely your personal preferences match up with the requirements and rewards associated with your chosen business, the greater the probability of your success. Finding a network marketing business that truly appeals to you and allows you to put your talents to good use is the first step. Deciding how much effort you want to put into the business and what you hope to get out of it is the next step. For example, one MLM opportunity may be fine as a sideline business that you can work on a few hours a week, while another calls for a full-time commitment. The earnings potential and other benefits (prestige, honors, and awards) to be gained must also be in line with your expectations.

The degree of risk involved in association with a company must be something you are comfortable with. Just as some entrepreneurs may relish the chance to get in on the "ground floor" with a new, unproven MLM company, others will opt for the security of joining a company that has already built up a name for itself.

Inasmuch as network marketing revolves around interpersonal relationships, another point to consider is the company's selling methods and whether or not you feel comfortable with them. If you would rather sell to prospective customers on a one-to-one basis, then a company that utilizes a "consultative" approach is the way to go. Conversely, if you prefer a group setting, then you're better off with a company that uses the "party plan" method, selling to friends in a host's or hostess's home, or "seminar" style presentations held in your home or a public meeting room.

The growing interest in network marketing has given rise to a wide variety of MLM companies from which to choose. By taking the time to explore the different network marketing opportunities that are available and your own needs, as well, you are bound to find a company that's right for you.

3

Getting Started

As a new distributor for an MLM company, there are certain steps that you should take to get your business off to a good start. Depending on what you sell and where your business is located, you will probably be required by the government to obtain various licenses and permits and to comply with certain regulations. You will want to decide on which legal form to use and the insurance coverage you will need. And, of course, you will want to set up an office, be it a corner or a whole room, large or small, at home or an outside location, so that you can work productively.

GOVERNMENT REGULATIONS

To protect your business's legal standing in the community, it is important to find out which local, state, and federal regulations apply to it.

Business Tax and Permit

Commonly referred to as a *business license,* this is issued by the city and/or county in which a business is located and is usually valid for one to two years. The fee for it, which is based on the gross sales of your business, can range from less than $50 to more than $150. To find out if a business license is necessary in your particular circumstances and/or which agency issues it, check the White Pages of your telephone directory under City of _____, Business Tax Division, Business Licenses, or City Clerk.

Fictitious Business Name Statement

In order to avoid having the public confuse independent distributors' businesses with the parent companies they represent, MLM companies have definite rules about how their corporate names can be used. The name "_____ Company, Inc., Your Name, Independent Representative" would normally be an acceptable name for your business since it indicates your independent status. At the same time, it tells the public that you own the business. If you're planning to operate your business under a name that doesn't include your name, such as "B & G Enterprises" or "The Nutrition Specialists," then you'll probably need to file a "fictitious business name statement" with the county clerk's office. The purpose of this statement is to inform the public of your identity and the identities of any others who are co-owners in the business.

Providing this public notice is a two-part process that

involves (1) filing the statement with the county clerk and (2) having the statement published in a newspaper of general circulation. You can usually eliminate the first part by going directly to the newspaper that's going to run your statement. As a convenience to their customers, most newspapers keep fictitious business name forms on hand (see the sample on page 28) and will file the completed statement for you. The total cost for filing and publishing the statement should be somewhere between $30 and $90.

Zoning Restrictions

If you're going to run your business out of your home, as the majority of network marketers do, then you'll need to find out what local zoning restrictions, if any, apply to a home business. Just as some people are more entrepreneurially inclined than others, so are some communities. Whereas one neighborhood may encourage home-based businesses, another may not. Elements of a business that are typically regulated include: the types of businesses that are acceptable, size and placement of signs, exterior merchandise displays, inventory storage, parking, and hours of operation. There may also be zoning restrictions limiting the number of employees you can hire or the number of attendees at presentations held in your home. In general, though, most home-based MLM businesses manage to operate alongside their neighbors without incident. To find out the zoning restrictions for your community, contact your local planning department or zoning board.

FICTITIOUS BUSINESS NAME STATEMENT

REMINDER
1. Submit original and 3 copies.
2. Filing fee $13.00 for one business name.
   $2.00 for each additional business name.
   $2.00 for each additional partner after first two.
3. Provide return stamped envelope if mailed.

☐ New Fictitious Business Name Statement

☐ Refile

GARY L. GRANVILLE
COUNTY CLERK
700 CIVIC CENTER DRIVE, WEST
P.O. BOX 838
SANTA ANA, CALIFORNIA 92702

THIS STATEMENT WAS FILED WITH THE COUNTY CLERK OF ORANGE COUNTY ON DATE INDICATED BY FILE STAMP BELOW.

FICTITIOUS BUSINESS NAME STATEMENT

File No. _____   THE FOLLOWING PERSON(S) IS (ARE) DOING BUSINESS AS: (TYPE ALL INFORMATION)

1.	Fictitious Business Name(s)
2.	Street Address, City & State of Principal place of Business in California — Zip Code
3.	Full name of Registrant — (if corporation—show state of incorporation)
	Residence Address — City — State — Zip Code
	Full name of Registrant — (if corporation—show state of incorporation)
	Residence Address — City — State — Zip Code
	Full name of Registrant — (if corporation—show state of incorporation)
	Residence Address — City — State — Zip Code
4.	(CHECK ONE ONLY) This business is conducted by ( ) an individual ( ) a general partnership ( ) a limited partnership ( ) an unincorporated association other than a partnership ( ) a corporation ( ) a business trust ( ) co-partners ( ) husband and wife ( ) joint venture ( ) other—please specify
5.	THE REGISTRANT(S) COMMENCED TO TRANSACT BUSINESS UNDER THE FICTITIOUS BUSINESS NAME(S) LISTED ABOVE ON: DATE: — THE FILING OF THIS STATEMENT DOES NOT OF ITSELF AUTHORIZE THE USE IN THIS STATE OF A FICTITIOUS BUSINESS NAME IN VIOLATION OF THE RIGHTS OF ANOTHER UNDER FEDERAL, STATE, OR COMMON LAW (SEE SECTION 14400 ET SEQ., BUSINESS AND PROFESSIONS CODE).
6.	Signature _____ (TYPE OR PRINT NAME) — If Registrant is a corporation sign below: Corporation Name _____ Signature & Title _____

NOTICE: This Fictitious Business Name Statement expires five (5) years from the date it was filed in the Office of the County Clerk.

FILE NO_____

FO182 266.10 (3/89)   FILE WITH COUNTY CLERK

Seller's Permit

Many states require anyone who buys and sells merchandise to obtain a seller's permit. This permit (1) exempts you from paying sales tax on the merchandise you purchase for resale through your business and (2) authorizes you to collect any sales tax from your customers. Depending on how your MLM company operates, a permit may or may not be necessary. To eliminate the need for each distributor to have a seller's permit, many MLM companies collect and pay any sales tax for their distributors. To get the details on this, check your company's policies and procedures manual. In the event that you do need to obtain a permit, there is no fee for it, although you may be asked to post a bond based on your estimated gross sales for the year. For more information on seller's permits, contact your state's tax board.

Occupational License

To maintain set standards of performance and protect the safety of consumers, most states regulate entry into specific occupations or professions, such as those in the health services, cosmetology, accounting, and real estate fields. If you will be working in a regulated field, you must first meet the standards set forth by the state licensing board governing your occupation. Once you have demonstrated your competence, you will be issued a license that is usually valid for a period of one to two years and is renewable. To determine if an occupational license is required for your type of network marketing activities, check with your state's Department of Consumer Affairs.

Employer Identification Number

If you employ one or more persons in your business, the federal government requires you to have an employer identification number. This enables the government to verify that you are paying all appropriate employer taxes and withholding the proper amounts from employee paychecks. Even though you probably won't have any employees in the beginning, it's still advisable to obtain a number, especially if you sell to businesses, because customers often need it for their records. And if you should decide to hire someone later, to take in a partner, or to incorporate your network marketing business, you will need the number for tax purposes. Obtaining your identification number is an easy matter. Just fill out IRS form number SS-4 as shown on the sample on page 31 and submit it to the Internal Revenue Service. There is no fee.

Consumer Protection Regulation

To protect the rights of consumers, the federal government regulates business practices in a variety of areas. Network marketing businesses that engage in mail-order sales or sell their products in more than one state are subject to regulation by the Federal Trade Commission, Interstate Commerce Commission, and/or the U.S. Postal Service. The Federal Trade Commission also oversees product packaging and labeling, product war-

APPLICATION FOR EMPLOYER IDENTIFICATION NUMBER

Form **SS-4** (Rev. August 1988) Department of the Treasury Internal Revenue Service	**Application for Employer Identification Number** (For use by employers and others. Please read the attached Instructions before completing this form.) Please type or print clearly.	Offical Use Only OMB No. 1545-0003 Expires 7-31-91

1 Name of applicant (True legal name. See instructions.)

2 Trade name of business if different from item 1	**3** Executor, trustee, "care of name"

4 Mailing address (street address) (room, apt., or suite no.)	**5** Address of business, if different from item 4. (See instructions.)

4a City, state, and ZIP code	**5a** City, state, and ZIP code

6 County and State where principal business is located

7 Name of principal officer, grantor, or general partner. (See instructions.) ▶

8 Type of entity (Check only one.) (See instructions.)

- ☐ Individual SSN_____
- ☐ Plan administrator SSN_____
- ☐ Partnership
- ☐ REMIC
- ☐ Personal service corp.
- ☐ Other corporation (specify)_____
- ☐ State/local government
- ☐ National guard
- ☐ Federal government/military
- ☐ Church or church controlled organization
- ☐ Other nonprofit organization (specify)_____ If nonprofit organization enter GEN (if applicable)_____
- ☐ Farmers' cooperative
- ☐ Estate
- ☐ Trust
- ☐ Other (specify) ▶

8a If a corporation, give name of foreign country (if applicable) or state in the U.S. where incorporated ▶

Foreign country	State

9 Reason for applying (check only one)

- ☐ Started new business
- ☐ Hired employees
- ☐ Created a pension plan (specify type) ▶_____
- ☐ Banking purpose (specify) ▶
- ☐ Changed type of organization (spec fy) ▶_____
- ☐ Purchased going business
- ☐ Created a trust (specify) ▶_____
- ☐ Other (specify) ▶

10 Business start date or acquisition date (Mo., day, year) (See instructions.)	**11** Enter closing month of accounting year (See instructions.)

12 First date wages or annuities were paid or will be paid (Mo., day, year). Note: If applicant is a withholding agent, enter date income will first be paid to nonresident alien. (Mo. , day, year). . . . . ▶

13 Enter highest number of employees expected in the next 12 months. Note: If the applicant does not expect to have any employees during the period, enter "0." . . . . ▶

Nonagricultural	Agricultural	Household

14 Does the applicant operate more than one place of business? . . . . ☐ Yes ☐ No
If "Yes," enter name of business. ▶

15 Principal activity or service (See instructions.) ▶

16 Is the principal business activity manufacturing?. . . . . ☐ Yes ☐ No
If "Yes," principal product and raw material used. ▶

17 To whom are most of the products or services sold? Please check the appropriate box.
☐ Business (wholesale)
- ☐ Public (retail)
- ☐ Other (specify) ▶
- ☐ N/A

18 Has the applicant ever applied for an identification number for this or any other business?. . . . . ☐ Yes ☐ No
Note: If "Yes," please answer items 18a and 18b.

18a If the answer to item 18 is "Yes," give applicant's true name and trade name, if different when applicant applied.

True name ▶   Trade name ▶

18b Enter approximate date, city, and state where the application was filed and the previous employer identification number if known.

Approximate date when filed (Mo., day, year)	City, and state where filed	Previous EIN

Under penalties of perjury, I declare that I have examined this application, and to the best of my knowledge and belief, it is true, correct, and complete.

Telephone number (include area code)

Name and title (please type or print clearly) ▶

Signature ▶   Date ▶

Note: Do not write below this line.   For official use only.

Please leave blank ▶	Geo.	Ind.	Class	Reason for applying

For Paperwork Reduction Act Notice, see instructions.   ⬥ U.S. Government Printing Office: 1988-523-133/00332   Form **SS-4** (Rev. 8-88) ranties, and advertising claims. Nutritional supplements, health care products, and cosmetics are regulated by the Food and Drug Administration. Financial services businesses may come under the jurisdiction of the Securities and Exchange Commission. To familiarize yourself with the regulations that apply to your type of business, write to the Federal Trade Commission, Washington, DC 20580.

Trademarks, Patents, and Copyrights

In addition to protecting the rights of consumers, the federal government also protects the rights of entrepreneurs. In this case, it protects your right to use and profit from your own name (or business or product name), inventions, and artistic creations. More specifically, as a network marketer, it entitles you to benefit from the MLM company's name, inventions, and creations. These assets, when protected by trademark, patent, or copyright, can only be used by the MLM company itself and its authorized representatives, the independent distributors. This gives you a competitive edge over other businesses that don't have access to the MLM company's product offering or resources.

The following information should help to give you a better idea of the protection provided by trademarks, patents, and copyrights and the ways that you can use them to your advantage.

Trademarks

By definition, a trademark is any word, name, symbol, device, or combination thereof that is used to identify the products or services of a business and to distinguish them from those of other enterprises. Often one of an MLM company's (or any business's) most valuable assets, a trademark can help to define its image, increase customer awareness, and stimulate repeat purchases. Although a business isn't required by law to register its trademark, this is advisable since it offers the greatest protection. You register a trademark by completing the form on pages 34 and 35. Once a trademark is registered, the holder's right to use it extends for a period of ten years, at which time registration is renewable. For more information on trademarks, write to the U.S. Department of Commerce, Patent and Trademark Office, Washington, DC 20231, and ask them to send you their pamphlet "General Information Concerning Trademarks."

Patents

In granting a patent to a business, the federal government gives it the right to exclude all others from making, using, or selling its invention in the United States. Patents for new and useful products or processes are valid for 17 years. A design patent, covering only the style or appearance of a product, may be valid for a period ranging from $3^1/2$ to 14 years. Thus, if the MLM company you represent has patented products or processes, or should develop any in the future, the company and its distributors would have the exclusive right to them. If, in the course of running your network marketing business, you happen to develop a product, process, or design that has commercial possibilities, you can apply for patent protection, too. To get the basic facts on obtaining a patent, read "Patents and Inventions: An Information Aid for Inventors," which is avail-

TRADEMARK APPLICATION FORM

TRADEMARK APPLICATION, PRINCIPAL REGISTER, WITH DECLARATION (Partnership)	**MARK** *(identify the mark)*
	CLASS NO. *(if known)*

TO THE COMMISSIONER OF PATENTS AND TRADEMARKS:

NAME OF PARTNERSHIP

NAMES OF PARTNERS

BUSINESS ADDRESS OF PARTNERSHIP

CITIZENSHIP OF PARTNERS

The above identified applicant has adopted and is using the trademark shown in the accompanying drawing[1] for the following goods: _____

and requests that said mark be registered in the United States Patent and Trademark Office on the Principal Register established by the Act of July 5, 1946.

The trademark was first used on the goods[2] on _____ ; was first used on the goods[2] in
(date)

_____ commerce[3] on _____ ; and is now in use in
(type of commerce) *(date)*
such commerce.

4

The mark is used by applying it to[5] _____

and five specimens showing the mark as actually used are presented herewith.

6

_____
(name of partner)

being hereby warned that willful false statements and the like so made are punishable by fine or imprisonment, or both, under Section 1001 of Title 18 of the United States Code and that such willful false statements may jeopardize the validity of the application or any registration resulting therefrom, declares that he/she is a partner of applicant partnership; he/she believes said partnership to be the owner of the trademark sought to be registered; to the best of his/her knowledge and belief no other person, firm, corporation, or association has the right to use said mark in commerce, either in the identical form or in such near resemblance thereto as may be likely, when applied to the goods of such other person, to cause confusion, or to cause mistake, or to deceive; the facts set forth in this application are true; and all statements made of his/her own knowledge are true and all statements made on information and belief are believed to be true.

_____
(signature of partner)

_____
(date)

Form PTO - 1477 (4 - 82)   *(Instructions on reverse side)*   Patent and Trademark Office - U.S. DEPT. of COMMERCE
(over)

TRADEMARK APPLICATION FORM
(continued)

REPRESENTATION

If the applicant is not domiciled in the United States, a domestic representative must be designated. See Form 4.4.

If applicant wishes to furnish a power of attorney, see Form 4.2. An attorney at law is not required to furnish a power.

FOOTNOTES

1   If registration is sought for a word or numeral mark not depicted in any special form, the drawing may be the mark typed in capital letters on letter-size bond paper; otherwise, the drawing should be made with india ink on a good grade of bond paper or on bristol board.

2   If more than one item of goods in a class is set forth and the dates given for that class apply to only one of the items listed, insert the name of the item to which the dates apply.

3   Type of commerce should be specified as "interstate," "territorial," "foreign," or other type of commerce which may lawfully be regulated by Congress. Foreign applicants relying upon use must specify commerce which Congress may regulate, using wording such as commerce with the United States or commerce between the United States and a foreign country.

4   If the mark is other than a coined, arbitrary or fanciful mark, and the mark is believed to have acquired a secondary meaning, insert whichever of the following paragraphs is applicable:

  a) The mark has become distinctive of applicant's goods as a result of substantially exclusive and continuous

  use in _____ commerce for the five years next preceding the date of filing
  (type of commerce)
  of this application.

  b) The mark has become distinctive of applicant's goods as evidenced by the showing submitted separately.

5   Insert the manner or method of using the mark with the goods, i.e., "the goods," "the containers for the goods," "displays associated with the goods," "tags or labels affixed to the goods," or other method which may be in use.

6   The required fee of $175.00 for each class must be submitted. (An application to register the same mark for goods and/or services in more than one class may be filed; however, goods and/or services and dates of use, by class, must be set out separately, and specimens and a fee for each class are required.)

able from the U.S. Department of Commerce, Patent and Trademark Office, Washington, DC 20231.

Copyrights

A copyright protects the right of an individual to keep others from copying his or her creations. Although most commonly associated with literary works, copyright protection extends to graphic designs, paintings, sculpture, musical compositions, sound recordings, and audiovisual works. A business doesn't have to be in the arts to benefit from this protection. A sampling of the works that come within the broad scope of copyright coverage includes: brochures, catalogs and advertising copy, newsletters and books, audiocassettes and video tapes, reports, charts and technical drawings, and computer programs. Thus, the training and marketing materials the MLM company creates for its distributors, and any materials you create yourself, can be copyrighted.

Obtaining a copyright is relatively simple. All you need to do is provide public notice of the copyright on the work itself (e.g., © 19__ MLM Co.) and file an application form (as shown on pages 38 and 39). The fee is currently $20, and, once granted, the copyright is good for up to 50 years after the holder's death. For more information, or a copyright form itself, write to the Copyright Office, Library of Congress, Washington, DC 20559. Be sure to specify the type of work you want to copyright.

LEGAL FORM

Part of getting started as a network marketer involves choosing the legal structure you want to use for your

business: a sole proprietorship, partnership, or corporation. This is an important decision, since your choice of
legal structure will affect the taxes you pay, your decision-making authority, borrowing power, liability for
debts, and the very lifespan of the business. There's no
"one-size-fits-all" legal form that's right for every business,
so you'll have to consider the pros and cons of each to
choose the form that works best for you.

Sole Proprietorship

A business owned by one person, who is entitled to all
of its profits and responsible for all of its debts, is considered a sole proprietorship. Providing maximum
control and minimum government interference, this
legal form is currently used by more than 75 percent of
all businesses. The main advantages that differentiate
the sole proprietorship from other legal forms are (1)
the ease with which it can be started, (2) the owner's
freedom to make decisions, and (3) the distribution of
profits (owner takes all).

Still, the sole proprietorship isn't without disadvantages, the most serious of which is its unlimited liability.
As a sole proprietor, you are responsible for all business
debts. Should these exceed the assets of your business,
your creditors can claim your personal assets—home,
automobile, savings account, investments, and so forth.
Sole proprietorships also tend to have difficulty obtaining capital and holding on to key employees. This stems
from the fact that sole proprietorships generally have
fewer resources and offer less opportunity for job ad-
vancement. Thus, anyone who chooses the sole proprietorship should be prepared to be a generalist, per-

COPYRIGHT APPLICATION FORM

FORM TX
UNITED STATES COPYRIGHT OFFICE

REGISTRATION NUMBER

TX   TXU

EFFECTIVE DATE OF REGISTRATION

Month   Day   Year

DO NOT WRITE ABOVE THIS LINE. IF YOU NEED MORE SPACE, USE A SEPARATE CONTINUATION SHEET.

1

TITLE OF THIS WORK ▼

PREVIOUS OR ALTERNATIVE TITLES ▼

PUBLICATION AS A CONTRIBUTION If this work was published as a contribution to a periodical, serial, or collection, give information about the collective work in which the contribution appeared. **Title of Collective Work ▼**

If published in a periodical or serial give: Volume ▼	Number ▼	Issue Date ▼	On Pages ▼

2

a

NAME OF AUTHOR ▼

DATES OF BIRTH AND DEATH
Year Born ▼   Year Died ▼

Was this contribution to the work a "work made for hire"?
☐ Yes
☐ No

AUTHOR'S NATIONALITY OR DOMICILE
Name of Country
OR { Citizen of ▶_____
Domiciled in ▶_____

WAS THIS AUTHOR'S CONTRIBUTION TO THE WORK
Anonymous? ☐ Yes ☐ No
Pseudonymous? ☐ Yes ☐ No
If the answer to either of these questions is "Yes," see detailed instructions.

NATURE OF AUTHORSHIP Briefly describe nature of the material created by this author in which copyright is claimed. ▼

NOTE

Under the law, the "author" of a "work made for hire" is generally the employer, not the employee (see instructions). For any part of this work that was "made for hire" check "Yes" in the space provided, give the employer (or other person for whom the work was prepared) as "Author" of that part, and leave the space for dates of birth and death blank.

b

NAME OF AUTHOR ▼

DATES OF BIRTH AND DEATH
Year Born ▼   Year Died ▼

Was this contribution to the work a "work made for hire"?
☐ Yes
☐ No

AUTHOR'S NATIONALITY OR DOMICILE
Name of country
OR { Citizen of ▶_____
Domiciled in ▶_____

WAS THIS AUTHOR'S CONTRIBUTION TO THE WORK
Anonymous? ☐ Yes ☐ No
Pseudonymous? ☐ Yes ☐ No
If the answer to either of these questions is "Yes," see detailed instructions.

NATURE OF AUTHORSHIP Briefly describe nature of the material created by this author in which copyright is claimed. ▼

c

NAME OF AUTHOR ▼

DATES OF BIRTH AND DEATH
Year Born ▼   Year Died ▼

Was this contribution to the work a "work made for hire"?
☐ Yes
☐ No

AUTHOR'S NATIONALITY OR DOMICILE
Name of Country
OR { Citizen of ▶_____
Domiciled in ▶_____

WAS THIS AUTHOR'S CONTRIBUTION TO THE WORK
Anonymous? ☐ Yes ☐ No
Pseudonymous? ☐ Yes ☐ No
If the answer to either of these questions is "Yes," see detailed instructions.

NATURE OF AUTHORSHIP Briefly describe nature of the material created by this author in which copyright is claimed. ▼

3

YEAR IN WHICH CREATION OF THIS WORK WAS COMPLETED This information must be given in all cases.
◀ Year

DATE AND NATION OF FIRST PUBLICATION OF THIS PARTICULAR WORK
Complete this information ONLY if this work has been published.
Month ▶_____ Day ▶_____ Year ▶_____
◀ Nation

4

See instructions before completing this space.

COPYRIGHT CLAIMANT(S) Name and address must be given even if the claimant is the same as the author given in space 2.▼

TRANSFER If the claimant(s) named here in space 4 are different from the author(s) named in space 2, give a brief statement of how the claimant(s) obtained ownership of the copyright.▼

APPLICATION RECEIVED

ONE DEPOSIT RECEIVED

TWO DEPOSITS RECEIVED

REMITTANCE NUMBER AND DATE

DO NOT WRITE HERE
OFFICE USE ONLY

MORE ON BACK ▶
• Complete all applicable spaces (numbers 5-11) on the reverse side of this page.
• See detailed instructions. • Sign the form at line 10.

DO NOT WRITE HERE

Page 1 of_____pages

38

COPYRIGHT APPLICATION FORM
(continued)

DO NOT WRITE ABOVE THIS LINE. IF YOU NEED MORE SPACE, USE A SEPARATE CONTINUATION SHEET.

PREVIOUS REGISTRATION Has registration for this work, or for an earlier version of this work, already been made in the Copyright Office?
☐ **Yes** ☐ **No** If your answer is "Yes," why is another registration being sought? (Check appropriate box) ▼
☐ This is the first published edition of a work previously registered in unpublished form.
☐ This is the first application submitted by this author as copyright claimant.
☐ This is a changed version of the work, as shown by space 6 on this application.
If your answer is "Yes," give: **Previous Registration Number ▼**   **Year of Registration ▼**

5

DERIVATIVE WORK OR COMPILATION Complete both space 6a & 6b for a derivative work; complete only 6b for a compilation.
a. Preexisting Material Identify any preexisting work or works that this work is based on or incorporates. ▼

b. Material Added to This Work Give a brief, general statement of the material that has been added to this work and in which copyright is claimed. ▼

See instructions
before completing
this space.

6

MANUFACTURERS AND LOCATIONS If this is a published work consisting preponderantly of nondramatic literary material in English, the law may
require that the copies be manufactured in the United States or Canada for full protection. If so, the names of the manufacturers who performed certain
processes, and the places where these processes were performed **must be given. See instructions for details.**
Names of Manufacturers ▼   **Places of Manufacture ▼**

7

REPRODUCTION FOR USE OF BLIND OR PHYSICALLY HANDICAPPED INDIVIDUALS   A signature on this form at space 10, and a
check in one of the boxes here in space 8, constitutes a non-exclusive grant of permission to the Library of Congress to reproduce and distribute solely for the blind
and physically handicapped and under the conditions and limitations prescribed by the regulations of the Copyright Office: (1) copies of the work identified in space
1 of this application in Braille (or similar tactile symbols); or (2) phonorecords embodying a fixation of a reading of that work; or (3) both.
  a ☐ Copies and Phonorecords   b ☐ Copies Only   c ☐ Phonorecords Only   See instructions.

8

DEPOSIT ACCOUNT If the registration fee is to be charged to a Deposit Account established in the Copyright Office, give name and number of Account.
Name ▼   **Account Number ▼**

9

CORRESPONDENCE Give name and address to which correspondence about this application should be sent. Name/Address/Apt/City/State/Zip ▼

Area Code & Telephone Number ▶

Be sure to
give your
daytime phone
◀ number.

CERTIFICATION* I, the undersigned, hereby certify that I am the   ☐ author
                                              Check one ▶ ☐ other copyright claimant
                                                           ☐ owner of exclusive right(s)
of the work identified in this application and that the statements made   ☐ authorized agent of _____
by me in this application are correct to the best of my knowledge.   Name of author or other copyright claimant, or owner of exclusive right(s) ▲

Typed or printed name and date ▼ If this is a published work, this date must be the same as or later than the date of publication given in space 3.
_____ date ▶ _____

Handwritten signature (X) ▼

10

* 17 U.S.C. § 506(e) Any person who knowingly makes a false representation of a material fact in the application for copyright registration provided for by section 409, or in any written statement filed in
connection with the application, shall be fined not more than $2,500.

☆U.S. GOVERNMENT PRINTING OFFICE: 1982-361-278/58

Sept. 1982—500,000

forming a variety of functions from accounting to advertising.

Partnership

A business owned by two or more people who agree to
share in its profits is considered a partnership. Like the
sole proprietorship, it is easy to start and the red tape
involved is usually minimal. The main advantages of the
partnership form are that the business can (1) draw on
the skills and abilities of each partner, (2) offer employees the opportunity to become partners, and (3) utilize
the partners' combined financial resources. However,
for your own protection, it is advisable to have a written
partnership agreement. This document should state (1)
each partner's rights and responsibilities, (2) the amount
of capital each partner is investing in the business, (3)
the method for distribution of profits, (4) the procedure
to follow if a partner joins or leaves the business, and
(5) how the assets are to be divided if the business is
discontinued.

Partnerships also have their share of disadvantages.
The unlimited liability that applies to sole
proprietorships is even worse for partnerships. As a
partner, you are responsible not only for your own
business debts, but for those of your partner(s) as well.
Should they incur debts or legal judgments against the
business, you could be held legally responsible for them.
Disputes among partners can be a problem, too. Unless
you and your partner(s) can see eye to eye on how the
business should be run and what it should accomplish,
you could have a troublesome relationship.

THE ADVANTAGES AND DISADVANTAGES OF EACH LEGAL FORM OF OWNERSHIP

Sole Proprietorship

Advantages	Disadvantages
• You're the boss.	• You assume unlimited liability.
• It's easy to get started.	
• You keep all profits.	• The amount of investment capital you can raise is limited.
• Income from business is taxed as personal income.	
	• You need to be a generalist.
• You can discontinue your business at will.	• Retaining high-caliber employees is difficult.
	• The life of the business is limited.

Partnership

Advantages	Disadvantages
• Two heads are better than one.	• Partners have unlimited liability.
• It's easy to get started.	• Partners must share all profits.
• More investment capital is available.	• Partners may disagree.
• Partners pay only personal income tax.	• The life of the business is limited.
• High-caliber employees can be made partners.	

Corporation

Advantages	Disadvantages
• Stockholders have limited liability.	• Corporations are taxed twice.
• Corporations can raise the most investment capital.	• Corporations must pay capital stock tax.
• Corporations have unlimited life.	• Starting a corporation is expensive.
• Ownership is easily transferable.	• Corporations are closely regulated by government agencies.
• Corporations utilize specialists.	

Corporation

A corporation differs from the other legal forms of business in that the law regards it as an artificial being that possesses the same rights and responsibilities as a person. Unlike sole proprietorships or partnerships, it has an existence separate from its owners. As a result, the corporation offers some unique advantages, including: (1) limited liability (owners are not personally responsible for the debts of the business), (2) the ability to raise capital by selling shares of stock, and (3) easy transfer of ownership from one individual to another. And, unlike the sole proprietorship and partnership, the corporation has "unlimited life" and, thus, the potential to outlive its original owners.

The main disadvantages of the corporate form can be summed up in two words: taxation and complexity. In what amounts to double taxation, you must pay taxes on both the income the corporation earns and the income you earn as an individual. Corporations are also required to pay an annual tax on all outstanding shares of stock. Given its complexity, a corporation is both more difficult and more expensive to start than are the sole proprietorship and the partnership. In order to form a corporation, you must be granted a charter by the state in which your business is located. For a small business, the cost of incorporating usually ranges from $500 to $2,000. This includes the costs for legal assistance in drawing up your charter, state incorporation fees, and the purchase of record books and stock certificates. And, since corporations are subject to closer regulation by the government, the owners must bear the ongoing cost of preparing and filing state and federal reports.

S Corporation

If you are interested in forming a corporation but hesitate to do so because of the double taxation, there is a way to avoid it. You can do this by making your business an S corporation. The Internal Revenue Service permits this type of corporation to be taxed as a partnership rather than as a corporation. However, in order to qualify for S status, your business must meet the specific requirements set forth by the IRS. These include limits on (1) the number and type of shareholders in the business, (2) the stock that is issued, and (3) the corporation's sources of revenues. For more information on forming an S corporation, ask the IRS for its free publication, *Tax Guide for Small Business,* publication number 334.

In evaluating the merits of the different legal forms, it's a good idea to confer with the MLM company's legal department and/or your own attorney to get additional input. Depending on the policies and procedures of the company you represent, there may be certain restrictions on the type of legal form you can use, or there may be advantages associated with one form but not another.

INSURANCE COVERAGE

There's no point in working to build your business if you don't take adequate measures to protect it. What would you do if there were an accident? if a burglar broke in and stole your merchandise or office equipment? if a dissatisfied customer decided to sue? if you became ill or disabled and couldn't work?

To deal with these and other hazards associated with running a network marketing business, it's important to evaluate the risks involved and to obtain the necessary insurance coverage.

Homeowner's Insurance

If your business is located at home, one of the first things you should do is check to see what kind of coverage, if any, is extended to the business under your homeowner's or renter's policy. For example, some policies cover business furnishings and equipment as a matter of course. Other policies do not. Also, one policy may protect you from personal liability if a business visitor is injured in your home, while another policy will not.

It's important to find out what's covered and what's not. At the same time, you want to make sure that you don't inadvertently void your policy by using your home to conduct business. Some homeowner's polices have a clause that forbids working at home. By checking with your insurance carrier before you start, you can determine if your business activities are compatible with the terms of your policy. Then, depending on the circumstances, you can make the appropriate arrangements— updating, expanding, or replacing the policy—to obtain the amount of coverage you require.

Adding a "business option" rider to your existing homeowner's policy may be the answer. For a few dollars more per year, a business option typically reimburses you for damages or loss to business property and extends your homeowner's liability coverage to include business-related injuries. To find out more about this option and what it provides, talk to your insurance agent.

Even the most comprehensive homeowner's policy cannot protect you against everything. In order to adequately safeguard yourself and your business, you should find out about the other kinds of insurance that are available and choose the coverage that suits your needs.

Fire Insurance

If you have an outside office or a warehouse for storing inventory, then you'll need to obtain fire insurance. Fire insurance protects your building and the property contained within it against damage inflicted by fire or lightning. Standard fire insurance policies do not cover accounting records, securities, deeds, money, bills, or manuscripts. Nor do they protect you against smoke or water damage that occurs as a result of a fire. To guard excluded valuables and to protect against these exempted hazards, additional coverage is needed.

Automobile Insurance

Any automobiles or trucks that you use in your network marketing business must be insured. And it is important to get coverage that protects you not just against property damage to the vehicle, but also against bodily injury claims and the actions of uninsured motorists

Crime Insurance

To protect your property against thefts not covered under your homeowner's insurance policy, you may also need to obtain some form of crime insurance. The most popular form is the *comprehensive insurance policy:* a sort of all-in-one policy that protects you against burglaries, robberies, and a variety of related hazards.

Liability Insurance

As a network marketer, you are responsible for the safety of your customers, network members, and employees in conjunction with their business dealings with you.

To protect yourself accordingly, you may want to purchase one or more of the following types of liability insurance:

- *General Liability Insurance.* The most far-reaching type of liability insurance available, it provides basic coverage against all liabilities not specially excluded from the policy.
- *Product Liability Insurance.* This insurance protects you against financial loss in the event that someone is injured by a product you manufacture or distribute.
- *Professional Liability Insurance.* For doctors, lawyers, consultants, and others who provide advice or information or perform a service, this insurance protects against damages claims brought by dissatisfied clients.

Personal Insurance

Personal insurance protects both you and any employees you may have against personal loss resulting from accident or injury. Health insurance, disability insurance, and worker's compensation all contribute to this protection. Note that employers are required by law to have worker's compensation insurance to cover damages arising from on-the-job injuries or occupational diseases.

Insurance needs vary widely from one network marketing business to the next. The best way to determine the types of insurance that you should buy is to discuss your situation with an insurance professional.

FURNISHINGS AND EQUIPMENT

Setting up your office space doesn't have to be an elaborate or costly production. Through careful planning, you can create a work environment that is both attractive and efficient, and still stay within your budget.

Whether you decide to work out of your home or another location, you will need some basic office furnishings and equipment. And while you don't need to purchase everything at once, you do want to have what you will need to be properly organized and to be able to interact with customers and network members, to process orders and service accounts, and to store and display merchandise. Among the essentials are:

- Desk, or worktable, and chair
- Guest chairs (2)
- Filing cabinet
- Storage/display shelves
- Bulletin board
- Telephone
- Answering machine
- Typewriter (or word processor or computer with a printer)
- Calculator

You might decide to purchase more expensive items like the following when your business is making a profit and when you feel a need for them. These items include:

- Personal computer
- Fax machine
- Photocopy machine
- Video tape player

These items are far from being an extravagance. A computer can save time and money by enabling you to monitor expenses and sales revenues, maintain customer files and mailing lists, track inventory, prepare letters and reports, and design graphics for brochures and presentation materials. And, since computers are becoming increasingly affordable, they aren't just for "Big Business" anymore. Both a fax machine and a photocopy machine can speed up order processing and assist you in communicating with network members. A videotape player can come in handy during sales presentations, opportunity meetings, and training sessions. The MLM company you represent will most likely have video tapes that you can use, or you can create your own tapes.

If your goal is to furnish your business as inexpensively as possible, there are several ways to accomplish this. Look for sales at office furniture and electronic stores, and investigate auctions, surplus outlets, discount stores, and newspaper classified ads. You might even create a desk or worktable yourself by placing two filing cabinets parallel to each other and covering them with a large piece of laminated countertop, a flush door, or wood that has been stained or painted. Industrial units made of bolted-together metal shelves and struts are not only economical, but are perfect for displaying merchandise or storing inventory. What is more, they can be painted to go with your color scheme. Another way to save money is to rent, or lease to own, items like a photocopy machine.

What counts isn't how much money you spend on your office or the number of electronic gadgets you have, but how appropriate everything is for your needs.

4

Developing Your Marketing Plan

In order to succeed as a network marketer, you need to identify potential customers and to develop an overall strategy for keeping them informed about what your business has to offer. In short, what is needed is a marketing plan.

DEFINING YOUR TARGET MARKET

To make the most of your network marketing opportunity, start by asking yourself "Who will buy from me?" The answer will come from some closer analysis.

- Will my products or services be used primarily by adults or children? men or women? married or single people?
- Will the purchase decision be made by one person? a couple? a committee?
- From what income level and age group will my customers come?

- What do my customers do for a living?
- Do my customers spend their leisure time reading? jogging? cooking? traveling? gardening? camping? playing tennis?

The more you know about your customers, the better. This information will make it easier for you to reach them and to fill their needs as well. If you're selling to a business rather than an individual, the same principle is true, except that you'll be learning as much as possible about the function of the business, its requirements, budget limitations, and purchasing procedures.

To determine which people or businesses make up your *target market*—the ones most likely to buy what you have to sell—you will need to do some marketing research. This means gathering customer information from such sources as:

- Personal observation
- The MLM company
- The government
- Chambers of commerce
- Trade associations
- The media

Personal Observation

Your marketing research should begin with your own personal observations of the customers who already buy from the MLM company you represent. By attending sales presentations held by your sponsor and other distributors, you can see the people who are there and listen to what they have to say.

- What specific needs do they have?
- What are they looking for?
- Which products are the most popular? the least popular?
- How much is the average sale?
- Which customers spend the most?

As you piece together your observations, you should be able to quickly get a feel for the market and the types of people who will be your customers.

The MLM Company

The MLM company you join is certain to have marketing research data on its customers. Much of this information will be contained in the company's handbook and its marketing and training materials. Study everything carefully. By familiarizing yourself with the literature and audio/video tapes the company provides to distributors, you'll be able to focus in on your target market more clearly and more quickly.

The Government

Government agencies at the federal, state, and local levels compile statistical data about consumer spending habits, sales trends, changes in the population, and so on. This information, which the government makes available to the public at little or no cost through reports and periodicals, can also help you to gauge the demand for your particular product. Those agencies offering the most useful information for identifying your target market include the Department of Commerce, the Small Business Administration, and the Economic Development Office. Most of the information you need should be in the reference section of your local library. You can also obtain it by writing to the specific agencies.

Chambers of Commerce

Your local chamber of commerce is another source of customer information that you should utilize. Established and operated by members of the business community, each chamber's goal is to promote and protect local business interests. As such, the chamber should be able to provide you with marketing research data pertaining to your particular business, along with the opportunity to meet with other local business persons.

Trade Associations

Trade associations, like chambers of commerce, can help you to get a better handle on your target market. Representing specific industries (arts and crafts, direct marketing, floristry, jewelry, real estate), trade associations provide industry members with a means of sharing ideas and information. Consumer profiles, forecasts of future demand levels and trends, and studies on the impact of proposed changes in government regulations are examples of the type of customer data available. To obtain information on trade associations or to find out which ones represent your industry, write to the American Society of Association Executives, 1575 I Street NW, Washington, DC 20003.

The Media

The media (including newspapers, magazines, radio, and television) are vital channels of communications, not only for promoting your business but also for obtaining information about your customers. Paying close attention to those articles and programs featuring or directed at your target market ("Women at Work," "Computer Update," "50 Dream Vacations," and so forth) should enable you to detect changes in the economy, customer needs, or current shopping patterns. What is more, following the advertisements is a good way to keep track of competitors' offerings and promotional strategies. Thus, one step in your marketing research should be to discover which media are most frequently used by your customers—and then tune in.

Once you've done your initial marketing research, you can begin to create a *customer profile* of the people in your target market. The Customer Profile chart on page 56 shows the types of personal and product-related data that you need to know in order to identify potential customers, or "prospects."

GENERATING LEADS

Knowing the types of people you want to sell to is one thing. Actually having *leads*—specific people in mind to contact—is something else. To generate leads, you're going to have to do some digging, starting with the people you already know and working from there.

The first thing you should do is write down the names of any relatives, friends, neighbors, or co-workers you think would be good prospects for your products or

CUSTOMER PROFILE

Personal Data

Sex	Male, female
Age range	Under 21, 22-34, 35-49, 50-64, 65+
Average household income	Under $15,000, $16,000–$25,000, $26,000–$35,000, $36,000–$50,000, $51,000–$74,000, $75,000+
Marital status	Single, married, widowed, divorced
Number of children	0, 1, 2, 3, 4, 5+
Stage in family life cycle	Single Married without children Married with preschool children Married with grammar school children Married with teenagers Married with older children at home Married "empty nesters" Single parents
Occupation	Blue collar, clerical, technical, managerial, professional, homemaker, retired
Education	Less than high school, high school, college
Location	City, suburb, country
Interests/Hobbies	Family, health and fitness, sports, arts, business, travel, computers, etc.
Personality	Quiet, gregarious

Product Data

Benefits desired	Economy, convenience, status, well-being
Usage rate	Order size, number of purchases
Brand loyalty	Low, medium, high
Key purchase factors	Price, quality, style, variety, service

services. Then expand your list to include people you do business with, members of organizations you belong to, former classmates, new people you meet professionally or socially—anyone you believe would benefit from your product offering. Using *leads worksheets* like the one shown on page 58 will help you to stay organized.

As you begin to contact the people on your list, make sure to ask each one for referrals. Even if the person you talk to isn't interested in buying your product or joining your network, he or she may know someone who is. And that person, in turn, may know someone else. By asking for referrals in this way, you can continually generate new leads.

Another way to get additional leads is to identify any professional, civic, or social organizations whose members fit into your target market. Then contact each organization to find out if you can obtain its membership list. Many organizations make their lists available for free or for a rental fee. You may even want to join the organization yourself—assuming that's possible. This offers the added advantage of allowing you to get to know the members personally and to network with them on an ongoing basis.

As you follow leads and generate new ones, keep track of each contact you make. Your records can be on paper or entered into a computer. In either case, the information you want to include is shown in the *leads contact list* on page 59.

FOCUSING ON GOOD PROSPECTS

Having identified your target market and devised a strategy for generating leads, it is critical that you learn to recognize good prospects when you see them.

LEADS WORKSHEET

People to Contact

Relatives, friends, neighbors

1. _____
2. _____
3. _____
4. _____
5. _____
6. _____
7. _____
8. _____
9. _____
10. _____

Members of groups I belong to

1. _____
2. _____
3. _____
4. _____
5. _____
6. _____
7. _____
8. _____
9. _____
10. _____

Business associates

1. _____
2. _____
3. _____
4. _____
5. _____
6. _____
7. _____
8. _____
9. _____
10. _____

Other people I know

1. _____
2. _____
3. _____
4. _____
5. _____
6. _____
7. _____
8. _____
9. _____
10. _____

LEADS CONTACT LIST

| Date | Name and Address | Telephone | Referred by | Interests | | Comments | Follow-Up |
				Products Yes/No	Network Yes/No		

Who Is a Good Prospect?

A prospect is any individual, group, or business that might be able to use what you have to sell. A *good* prospect, however, can use what you have to sell and, as shown in the chart on page 61, has three other characteristics: (1) a need for your product, (2) the means to afford it, and (3) the authorization to buy it. All three characteristics must be present. If any one of them is missing, your sale probably won't succeed. Or, if you do make the sale, you may have difficulty in getting paid later.

You want to use your resources of time and money effectively. This means you shouldn't waste them trying to sell to bad prospects. Therefore, it is in your best interest to identify the good prospects as quickly as possible by getting answers to the following questions:

1. *Does the prospect need my product?* The most basic rule of selling is "Find a need and fill it." Your first priority should be to determine if a prospect has a need for your product or service. Will using it enable the prospect to save or make money? increase efficiency? look or feel better? enjoy life more? get respect from others? The greater the prospect's need for the purchase, the better your chances of making the sale. For instance, a health-conscious individual might have a need for nutritious foods, vitamins, exercise equipment, or membership in a health club, not to mention the proper clothing to show off his or her body. A business that wants to be profitable might need anything from new equipment to a training program for its employees or an improved accounting system.

2. *Can the prospect afford my product?* There's no point in trying to sell something to a prospect who is unable

YOUR TARGET MARKET

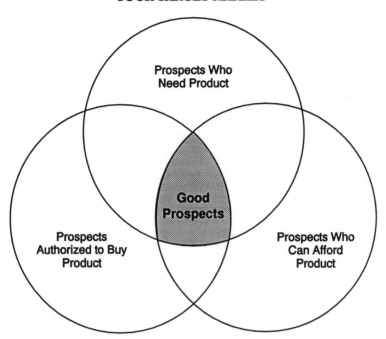

to pay for it. As much as the prospect might want or need what you have to offer, the need alone isn't enough to justify your sales effort. Even if you succeed in making the sale, you could easily end up with nothing more than a bad debt to show for it.

When a prospect's finances are questionable, proceed with caution—protect yourself, for example, by requiring payment in cash or cashier's check or money order, limiting the order quantity, or avoiding the sale altogether. If your MLM company permits you to accept payment by bank credit card, make sure that you obtain all the necessary information and that the card is valid.

3. Is the prospect authorized to buy my product? In your eagerness to answer the first two questions, don't overlook this equally important one. Just because a prospect needs and can afford a product doesn't mean the prospect is authorized to buy it. For instance, a child may feel that he or she "needs" to join a horror story book club, and the child may even have the money to buy the initial book. But the actual authority to join the club could very well rest with the child's parents, who have the final say on whether or not they can afford the club. Married couples often share the authority to make major purchases, such as new furniture, insurance, a computer, or a vacation. And, in selling to businesses, you'll find that the authority to buy can be spread out over different departments and levels of management. On important purchases, it is not uncommon for a dozen or more persons to be involved in the buying decision.

When more than one individual is involved in the buying decision, it's usually better to have all parties present for your sales presentation. You should also try to determine which individual will make the final decision. This is the person to whom you want to direct the most attention during the sales presentation.

PROMOTING YOUR BUSINESS

In addition to generating leads through personal contacts, there are other channels of communication that you can use—namely, publicity and advertising—to spread the word about your network marketing business.

Publicity refers to any *nonpaid* form of mass communication that you use to promote your business. It entails getting information about what you do or about your products or services reported in the news media. Such coverage is provided free of charge when the information is thought to have news value or to be of interest to the public. Publicity can best be characterized by its *three Cs:* cost, control, and credibility. As noted, there is no *cost* to you for the media coverage you receive. At the same time, however, you have no *control* over the nature of what that coverage will be. Publicity can be favorable or unfavorable—as likely to point out your business's problems as its accomplishments. It's this very lack of control, though, that gives publicity its greatest strength—*credibility.* The fact that it is the news media, rather than an advertiser, delivering the message makes it more believable.

Advertising refers to any *paid* form of mass communication that you use to promote your business. In general, it involves the purchasing of print space or air time in communication media (magazines, radio) or the using of direct mail or various "supplemental" means (brochures, gifts, samples) to reach your target market. Though advertising is recognized as a powerful business communication tool, network marketers often overlook it or don't know how to use it. This is unfortunate since advertising is the only communication method that gives you total control over the information that is directed at your target audience.

Which is best—publicity or advertising? The answer is both. Relying on publicity alone will result in a promotional strategy that's lacking in continuity and control. On the other hand, if you only use advertising, you will miss out on the opportunity to get free media exposure for your business and to enhance its credibility.

Before you use either method, though, review your company's policies and procedures manual to determine its guidelines on how representatives may promote their businesses. MLM companies generally have restrictions on how their names or logos may be used, what advertising materials—both company-created and representative-created—may be used, and what product claims may be made. There may also be restrictions governing your choice of media or publicity activities.

To avoid running into problems or jeopardizing your independent distributor status, it is best to discuss any promotional plans you have with the MLM company first. Together, you should be able to come up with a course of action that works for both of you.

The chart below shows the publicity and advertising methods that can be used to bolster your personal contact efforts. Depending on what network marketing business you're in, your target audience, and your budget and time limitations, some methods will be more suitable than others.

BUSINESS PROMOTION	
Publicity	*Advertising*
Presentations	Telephone book
Guest speaking	Direct mail
Awards	Flyers
Newsletters	Directory listings
Charitable donations	Newspapers
Timely events	Magazines
Human interest	Radio
Sponsorships	Television
	Sales promotion

Publicity

The following publicity methods can be used to obtain media exposure for your business. In deciding which ones to use, pick those that are most compatible with your own abilities and personal preferences.

Presentations

As a network marketer, much of what you do will center around the sales- and business-opportunity presentations you give to individuals and groups. Whenever a presentation is open to the public, one way to build attendance is to notify the local media of the event. This effort on your part can result in getting the presentation included in newspaper or radio-station Calendar of Events listings. To take advantage of this free media coverage, be sure to provide the date, time, place, and other relevant details. Be sure to get your notice in early enough (usually one to two weeks prior to the event) so that you don't miss the listing deadline.

Guest Speaking

In addition to the presentations you give, you might want to consider becoming a guest speaker for various groups. Business and social organizations are always looking for luncheon and dinner speakers on topics ranging from "Improving Your Time-Management Skills" to "Beauty on a Budget." By putting together a talk on a subject related to the products or services you sell, you can build a name for yourself and your company while generating sales leads and media coverage.

Awards

If you are fortunate enough to be honored through your work as a network marketer, your volunteer service to the community, or some other achievement, then you are news—news that results in publicity for you and more recognition of your name.

Newsletters

Another way to communicate with your target market and gain the attention of the media is to publish your own newsletter. Offering information of interest to current and prospective customers or network members, a newsletter is an excellent method for staying in contact with the people you want to reach. Your publication needn't be slick or expensive to produce. A computer-generated and photocopied newsletter consisting of two to four pages published bimonthly or quarterly would do the job. The important thing is that the information it provides is timely and of use to those who receive it.

Charitable Donations

One of the nicest ways to get publicity is by donating your products or services to a worthy cause. The people who receive your gift benefit and so do you. For instance, a network marketer in the children's toy field might donate products to a local school or youth group. Conversely, a representative for a cosmetics company could treat women at a senior citizens' center to a "day of beauty," providing skin treatments and manicures and free samples. These are the types of newsworthy stories that especially appeal to local newspapers and television news programs.

Timely Event

Staging a special event or presentation tied to a holiday or season is another means of getting the media's attention. If you can link your charitable donation to a timely event, such as Christmas, Mother's Day, or the World Series, so much the better. For example, a network marketer of crafts products could demonstrate how to make one-of-a-kind, personalized gifts for Christmas or Mother's Day.

Human Interest

Is there something unique, off-beat, or heart-warming about what you do or the type of network marketing business you're in? If so, you have a human interest story to offer to the public. A representative for a nutritional products company who also runs marathons would fit this category. So would a travel consultant who collects dolls from around the world or an insurance agent who writes detective fiction.

Sponsorships

Sports teams or individuals are always looking for sponsors. Your name or the name of your business could appear on the shirt of every child on a Little League team. You could be a contributing sponsor for a charitable event like a bike-a-thon or a walk-a-thon and have your name reach hundreds of people. A little investigation should uncover an outlet for your help.

Advertising

Each of the following advertising methods has its strengths and limitations. In choosing one medium or another, try to determine which one will enable you to reach your audience most effectively.

Telephone Book

One of the most widely used methods of advertising for promoting network marketing businesses is the telephone book. The main advantage of telephone-book advertising is its ability to reach people within a certain geographic area at the time when they want to buy. Having already recognized a need for a particular product or service, they are just looking for the right place to buy it. As such, your audience is "pre-sold."

A growing number of specialty directories add to the appeal of telephone-book advertising: "The Neighborhood Directory," "Silver Pages," "Business to Business Directory," and so on. Before you obtain a listing, be sure to check your company's guidelines on telephone-book advertising to determine the types of advertising formats that are approved for representatives. Your company may also stipulate which section to use (the White Pages or the Yellow Pages) and what category headings are appropriate.

Direct Mail

Direct mail advertising involves sending printed material, such as a letter, brochure, or catalog, through the mail to sales prospects or potential network members. Chief among direct mail's strengths are its selectivity and flexibility, which allow you to send any promotional message to anyone at any time. For example, you can use direct mail to:

- Reach new prospects
- Maintain customer contact

- Communicate with network members
- Announce new products or services
- Solicit mail-order business
- Solicit phone-order business

Direct mail does have a serious drawback, though. If you aren't careful, the people who receive your materials may regard them as junk mail and throw them away. Thus, your primary concern in using direct mail should be to get your advertisement into the right hands. The success of any direct-mail campaign rests squarely on the quality of its mailing list. The better your mailing list, the better the response to your advertisement.

To obtain a mailing list that works for you, you can either build your own list or buy one from a list broker. If you build the list yourself, some of the sources you can use are: your customer files, your customer-leads lists, business cards, organization directories, public announcements, and government records. For information on list brokers, check the Yellow Pages under "Mailing Lists" or consult the *Standard Rate and Data Service*, a monthly publication available at many libraries.

Flyers

A simple and inexpensive tool for promoting your business is the flyer. Flyers can be printed in varying quantities and distributed to pedestrians, office workers, spectators at sports events, shoppers, attendees at trade shows, or others in your target market. This method of advertising not only enables you to reach new prospects, but to do it on short notice. Since it isn't necessary to buy advertising space or to put together a mailing list, you can move quickly.

Before making your move, though, it is important to realize that not everyone appreciates being given a flyer. Building supervisors and groundskeepers may even prohibit the handing out of flyers because of the litter they create. The way to get around these obstacles is to make professional-looking flyers with clean graphics and understandable copy and to carefully select the people who are to receive them. For instance, participants at a 10-kilometer run should be likely prospects for nutrition and skin-care products.

Directory Listings

A number of publishing companies and trade and professional associations print directories that contain listings of individuals in various fields or types of businesses. For instance, there are directories that name people in such areas as financial planning, crafts, health and nutrition, security systems, and toys and gifts. Thus, depending on the type of network marketing business you're in, it may be possible to have your name included in one or more directories.

If you are contemplating obtaining a directory listing, first determine what the fee, if any, will be. Second, find out how many copies of the directory will be printed and who will receive them. After all, there's no benefit in being included in a directory that will only be seen by a few people or by people who are not in your target market.

Newspapers

Newspapers, the number-one media choice among advertisers large and small, are another promotional tool you may want to use, especially if your target market is your own community. When it comes to reaching a local audience, newspapers are hard to beat. Their readers are likely to be your potential customers and network members. Along with this, newspaper costs can usually be tailored to meet even a very limited budget. Keeping your ad small or placing your ad in the classified section of the paper lowers the price. Bear in mind, though, that readers often skip over ads without reading them. If your ad doesn't get their attention the first time, it probably never will, since newspapers are rarely kept more than a day or so.

To catch the reader's eye, it is essential to place your ad in the newspaper section (business, food, home, and so on) that is most often read by your prospects. Known as *preferred positioning*, this costs more, but it's worth it. Another way to get more benefits out of your newspaper advertising is to offer a discount to customers who mention seeing it or who redeem a coupon. This also tells you if your ad is working by allowing you to measure readers' response.

Magazines

The main advantage of magazines as a promotional vehicle is their selectivity. Given the large number of special-interest, trade, and professional magazines available, there's practically one for every audience. By choosing the magazines that focus on a topic of interest to your target market (money, health and fitness, food, travel, computers), you can get your message to the right people. Moreover, since people frequently save magazines for future reference after they've read them, magazine ads tend to have a long life span.

One disadvantage to magazines is that they have what's

known as a long *lead time*—the interval between when your ad is placed and when it actually appears. Magazine ads usually must be placed two or three months prior to publication. And, just as with newspapers, positioning is important to ensure that your ad is seen.

Radio

Radio, though not often used by network marketers, shouldn't be ignored entirely. It's practically everywhere that people are—at home or in the car, at work or on vacation—and 99 percent of all American households have at least one radio. Radio advertising offers a high degree of selectivity because different stations and programs appeal to different audiences.

The main drawbacks to radio advertising are its costs and complexity. The costs can be high because, to be effective, a commercial must be broadcast repeatedly over a period of weeks or months. You can minimize costs by advertising on smaller, less expensive stations—mainly the FM stations. Pooling resources with other network marketers in your area to pay for a combined commercial ("cooperative advertising") is another idea. Radio advertising can be complex because putting together a good commercial usually requires professional assistance. Fortunately, many radio stations are willing to help advertisers produce their commercials at little or no charge.

Television

Television, like radio, has generally been off limits to network marketers for much the same reasons of cost and complexity. But with 98 percent of all U.S. households having a television set and families watching an average of some seven hours of TV a day, it, too, is hard to ignore. Although the astronomical advertising rates of network television make it an unrealistic choice, the rates of *local, UHF,* and *cable* television may be affordable, particularly if you pool your resources with other network marketers, and these channels offer a greater degree of selectivity in reaching prospects.

Sales Promotion

Generally regarded as a supplement to traditional advertising, sales promotion is very well suited to the needs of network marketers. It includes such diverse promotion methods as business cards, brochures, advertising specialty items (pens, pencils, memo pads, and other objects imprinted with your name or message), and participation in trade shows. The practical-use specialty items should be particularly effective because they exert subtle advertising every time they are used.

Whatever combination of publicity and advertising you decide to use to promote your business, network marketing will always be at heart a people-powered activity. Promotion can help you to reach more people more often, but it is no substitute for personal contact and positive word-of-mouth communication. Ultimately, your success in multilevel marketing will depend on the lasting relationships you build with customers and network members.

5

Making the Sale

There's a saying in business that "Nothing happens until somebody sells something." To accomplish your goals in network marketing, you must be able to turn prospects into customers. Thus, having used your personal contacts and promotional skills to get the word out about what your business has to offer, you must now use selling skills to make the sale.

PLANNING YOUR SALES PRESENTATION

The secret of a successful sales presentation is planning. Instead of "winging it" or relying on "fast talking and fancy footwork" to get through sales presentations, the best salespersons *plan* their presentations carefully, anticipating the prospect's needs, budget, and willingness to buy. If you will be making your presentation to several people at once, then you will want to know as much about your audience as possible. This will enable you to focus on those things that have the greatest group appeal.

Once you have decided on the products or services you want to emphasize and the approach that will work best, you can begin to map out your presentation strategy. You need to plan what to say and what visual aids or demonstration techniques to use. None of these tasks is easy. Fortunately, as a network marketer, you have the advantage of being able to draw on the resources of the MLM company. By talking to other representatives and utilizing the company's sales and training materials, you can reduce your planning time and pick up valuable ideas.

Planning What to Say

In planning what to say in your sales presentation, your goal should be both to inform and to persuade. First, you want to provide the right amount and type of information so that the prospect knows what your network marketing business has to offer. Second, you want to present this information as persuasively as possible so that the prospect will be inclined to buy your product or service. To achieve this end, it helps to do the following:

- Make a list of the major points you want to cover in the sales presentation.
- Determine the approximate length of time you need to get your points across.
- Outline your presentation to see how everything fits together.
- Practice your presentation several times before actually trying it out on prospects. Recruit family members or friends to play the role of the prospect, and get their reactions.

- Don't try to memorize the presentation. A memorized speech will have a stilted, unnatural sound and make it difficult for you to interact with prospects. Copy your outline onto index cards, highlighting the outline with key words or phrases which you might memorize.
- While planning what to say, remember that it also pays to listen. This will enable you to create a more favorable impression and will help you to determine the prospect's needs.

If your MLM company provides representatives with sample scripts of presentations, this can be a big help. But every group and situation is different, so make sure that you tailor the script to match the circumstances of *your* presentation.

Using Visual Aids

Visual aids can make a sales presentation more interesting and help to hold the prospect's attention. What you use depends on the nature of your product or service, the location of the presentation, your audience, and your own preferences. The most obvious visual aid, of course, is the actual product that is for sale. Other visual aids include:

- Presentation folders
- Brochures
- Slides
- Videotapes
- Overhead projections
- Chalkboards

- Charts and graphs
- Photographs
- Posters
- Models
- Props

In putting together the visual elements of your presentation, check to see what materials are available from your company. If you can incorporate a company-produced slide show or video tape into your presentation, this will not only add to the presentation's visual impact, but will showcase the MLM company and its products in a favorable way.

As you're deciding what visual aids to use, don't fall into the trap of thinking that if one visual aid is good ten aids will be ten times as good. Too many visual aids can be both distracting and confusing. Charts and graphs should be clean and simple, with a minimum of lettering or numbers, so they do not become difficult to read and end up hurting your sales presentation. To help get organized for each presentation, try using a checklist like the one shown on page 79.

THE PRESENTATION

When you've reached the point at which you're ready to face the prospect, you can strengthen your sales presentation by being sure to (1) communicate clearly, (2) appeal to the prospect's five senses, (3) identify the prospect's needs, and (4) emphasize the benefits rather than just the features of your product.

PRESENTATION CHECKLIST

Date of Presentation _____

Person/Group I Will Be Seeing _____

Location _____

_____

Telephone Contact Number _____

Points to Cover	Visual Aids to Use
_____	_____
_____	_____
_____	_____
_____	_____
_____	_____

Meeting Room Arrangements _____

_____

_____

Equipment Needs _____

_____

_____

Things I Need to Do to Prepare for the Presentation

_____

_____

The Communication Process

The ability to communicate clearly is essential in giving a sales presentation. Before you can make the sale, you and the prospect must arrive at a meeting of the minds regarding what you are selling, its cost, the terms of the purchase, and so on. The only way for this meeting to take place is by communicating, or by sharing ideas and information.

As shown in the diagram of the communication process below, you must be able to get your sales points (message) across to the prospect and properly interpret the prospect's reactions to them (feedback).

Sending the Message

In sending your messages, it is important to speak clearly and distinctly and to use words that the prospect is likely to understand. Try to avoid obscure words, jargon, and

THE COMMUNICATION PROCESS

NOISE   NOISE

| Seller | Message Sent | Communication Channel | Message Received | Prospect |

NOISE   NOISE

FEEDBACK

technical terms unless you are certain that the prospect is familiar with them. Don't overlook the nonverbal message that you are sending, either. Otherwise, your body language (facial expressions, posture, gestures) could be telling the prospect something totally different from what you had planned. For example, slouching in your chair while telling a prospect about your attention to detail and insistence on quality will result in your sending two conflicting messages. Although your words are saying one thing, your body language is sending another message.

The Communication Channel

The communication channel itself is what brings you and the prospect together and enables both of you to send and receive messages. It can be a one-on-one meeting between you and the prospect, a meeting in which the prospect's family or business associates are present, or a group meeting with several different prospects in attendance. It can take place in a home, an office, a restaurant, a public meeting room, or some other convenient location.

Interpreting Feedback

Once the prospect has received your message, it's up to you to interpret the feedback that is generated. Is the prospect's response to your message positive or negative? What questions are raised? What doubts or uncertainties exist? Is the prospect eager or reluctant to buy from you?

Based on your interpretations of the feedback you receive, you can alter your sales presentation accordingly. The better you are at interpreting the prospect's messages, both verbal and nonverbal, the better you will be at making the sale.

Noise

The "noise" shown in the diagram of the communication process stands for anything that interferes with the exchange of information between you and the prospect. "Noise" could be the sound of people talking, a ringing phone, or equipment being operated, but it could also be the way you send your messages (using a poor choice of words, speaking too softly, mumbling). Sometimes speaking louder or explaining a sales point in a different way can compensate for actual noise. Other times you'll just have to do the best you can under the circumstances.

"Noise" could also stem from the way the prospect receives the messages (not hearing everything, daydreaming, misunderstanding what you said). Speaking louder may regain the prospect's attention, or you may have to change your way of presentation.

The Five Senses

One of the ways to increase the effectiveness of a sales presentation is to appeal to the prospect's five sense—the ability to hear, see, touch, smell, and taste. The more senses you can appeal to, the stronger your presentation will be. Instead of just talking to your prospects, you would do better to *show* them something or demonstrate something to them. And if you can get a prospect to touch, smell, or taste your product, that's even better. Of course, not every product or service can or should be made to appeal to all the senses. You would hardly expect a prospect to taste the shoe polish you're selling or to to touch something unpleasant. But, by directing your sales presentation to those senses to which your product does appeal, you can improve your success rate in making the sale.

Cosmetics, jewelry, and clothing are naturals for appealing to the five senses. Rather than just describing these products, a network marketer can let prospects see for themselves the difference a beauty product can make in their appearance or how an article of jewelry or clothing looks on them. With some creativity, even products or services that seem difficult to "showcase" in a concrete way *can* be made to appeal to the five senses. Consider, for example, insurance or financial investments. Since they are both intangible, you can't show or demonstrate them. But, you *can* show prospects pictures of smiling policy holders whose insurance got them through misfortune or of financially-secure investors enjoying the good life.

Prospects' Needs

By tuning into prospects' needs, you can focus your presentation on those points that are of the greatest importance to them. For example, suppose you are selling cookware. Depending on what the prospects' needs were, you could focus your presentation on the fact that the cookware would enable them to:

- Satisfy *time* needs: reduce cooking time
- Satisfy *health* needs: prepare nutritious meals
- Satisfy *relationship* needs: make family members' favorite dishes

- Satisfy *recognition* needs: impress guests with cooking ability
- Satisfy *creativity* needs: create new dishes

The ability to recognize and respond to prospects' needs is one of the most valuable skills a network marketer can possess. Instead of wasting time appealing to needs the prospect doesn't have, successful network marketers zero in on those needs that are not being currently fulfilled.

Benefits versus Features

Emphasizing benefits rather than features is another way to strengthen your sales presentations. While features describe a product or service, benefits represent the advantages the prospect will derive from the purchase. The essential difference, as shown in the chart on page 85, is that benefits give the prospect a reason to buy.

Your role as the seller is to convert features into benefits. Instead of focusing on what a product or service *is*, you want to focus on what it can *do* for the prospect. Once you've done that, you'll find that there's less possibility of the prospect saying "So what?" and a better chance that the response will be "That's great. I'll take it."

Using the AIDA Formula

In giving sales presentations, many sellers find that it also helps to follow a formula—specifically the AIDA

BENEFITS VERSUS FEATURES

Features	Benefits
These skin products contain special moisturizers.	You'll look younger.
These toys are recommended by educators.	Your child will do better in school.
The stone in this ring is a genuine sapphire.	This sapphire ring brings out the blue in your eyes.
This is an original oil painting.	No one else will own a work of art like this.
The money you invest in this fund is insured by the government.	Your money is safe.
This computer program is "user friendly."	You can start using the program immediately.
This is the best selection of needlepoint kits of any crafts company.	Now you can make one-of-a-kind gifts for your friends.
This line of security systems is state-of-the-art.	You won't have to worry about break-ins.
One of the advantages of our buyers service is its 800-number.	Everything you want is just a phone call away.
This glassware is the finest quality crystal.	Your friends will recognize your good taste.

formula. Consisting of four steps, this sales formula is designed to get the prospect's attention and then move the prospect to take action (make the purchase). As you can see, the formula's name is derived from the first letter of each of the steps involved in using it:

A Attention: The seller strives to gain the prospect's *attention* and to create an awareness of the products or services available.

I Interest: The seller stimulates the *interest* of the prospect by providing additional information.

D Desire: The seller arouses the prospect's *desire* to purchase the product or service by emphasizing its benefits.

A Action: The seller encourages the prospect to take *action* and buy.

Like shifting from one gear to another when driving a car, the transitions between steps in the AIDA formula should be smooth and natural. Once you've succeeded in getting the prospect's attention, you can begin to explain what your network marketing business has to offer.

HANDLING OBJECTIONS

Many sales experts insist that "the selling doesn't really begin until the customer says no." Instead of letting objections upset you or taking them personally, you should try to maintain a positive attitude. Accept the fact that a prospect's objections come with the territory. All sellers encounter them at one time or another. What separates the successful sellers from the rest is how they handle these objections.

Some of the most common objections prospects raise during sales presentations include:

1. I don't really need it right now.
2. I can't afford it.
3. It's overpriced.
4. This isn't what I had in mind.
5. I need more time to think about it.
6. I have to talk to my husband/wife first.
7. I already use a different brand.

Any one of these objections can effectively put an end to your sales presentation—if you let it. But by responding to the objection in a positive way and demonstrating that the benefits of the purchase outweigh the disadvantages, you still may be able to make the sale.

The following examples show how you can turn objections into orders:

1. *I don't really need it right now.*   If the prospect doesn't need what you are selling, there's nothing more to talk about, right? Not necessarily. Instead of accepting this objection at face value, try to determine whether or not a need really does exist. If, in your opinion, the prospect *does* need what you have to offer, then point this out:

"I can understand how a young person like yourself might feel that way about life insurance. Part of the beauty of this policy I'm suggesting, though, is that it's also a savings and investment plan that can provide you with extra income for a house, car, or those other major purchases you'll be making."

2. *I can't afford it.*   Ordinarily there is no point in continuing your sales presentation if the prospect really can't afford your products or services. However, if you're confident that the prospect *can* afford to buy, then you should explain how:

"Your reluctance to invest in a water purification system isn't surprising. With everything so expensive these days, why pay more for something that already comes out of your tap. But with all the impurities in the county water system, can you really afford not to give your family clean water to drink?"

3. *It's overpriced.*   This is a common objection voiced by prospects. But if you know for a fact that your price is in line with those of your competitors, draw this to the prospect's attention. On the other hand, if your price is higher, then discuss the reasons why:

"Yes, it's true that our products cost a little more. That's because all of our cookware goes through a rigorous testing process and comes with a lifetime warranty and a money-back guarantee."

4. *This isn't what I had in mind.*   Overcoming this objection can be a definite challenge, especially if you don't have anything else to offer the prospect. Don't give up, though. Find out what the prospect *was* expecting in the product or service you are selling; then try to capitalize on the differences.

"The doll *doesn't* talk, I know. But we made her that way in order to stimulate children's imaginations. Rather than being limited to a few phrases, our doll can say whatever your child wants her to say."

5. *I need more time to think about it.*   When a prospect raises this objection, your job is to find out *why* the prospect needs more time to make a decision. If the delay seems justified, you should go along with it and set up a specific date to get the prospect's answer. But if you think the prospect is really saying no, then emphasize the benefits again:

"I realize it isn't every day that you decide to have professional photographs taken of your family. With our special holiday rate, though, you will save money. What's more, if we go ahead and write up the order today, you can have the portraits in time for Christmas."

6. *I have to talk to my husband/wife first.* This is a tricky objection to overcome because it's hard to know if the prospect really does have to talk to his/her spouse or is simply stalling for time. In either case, the way to get around it is to reduce the risk associated with making the purchase:

"I can see where you would want to share a decision like this. Fortunately, you can cancel your membership in our buyers' service at any time—and only pay for the services you actually use. So there's no reason not to sign up now and take advantage of our special low rate."

7. *I already use a different brand.* Even the most loyal customer can usually be swayed by a better product offering. The best way to counter this objection is to prove that it would be to the customer's advantage to change brands. Here you can emphasize whatever it is (quality, price, durability, ease of usage, and so forth) that makes your product superior to the one the prospect is currently using:

"I'm familiar with the brand you're using and can understand your loyalty to it. But with our weight-loss food supplement, you'll get the same great taste without the bother. Each portion comes in a separate packet so there's no measuring to do and no mess."

CLOSING THE SALE

If the prospect is responding favorably to your presentation and appears ready to make a decision, just one thing remains—closing the sale. This is the moment when you actually ask the prospect to buy.

There are several ways to close a sale. The most frequently used methods include:

1. Asking for the order
2. Assuming the prospect will place the order
3. Giving the prospect a choice
4. Providing an added inducement to buy
5. Warning the prospect to buy before it's too late

1. *Asking for the order.*   The simplest, most direct way to close a sale is to ask the prospect to place an order. Rather than beating around the bush or backing into the close, this approach meets it head on:
- "Would you like me to go ahead and write up your order now?"
- "Now that you know what my service is all about, shall we go ahead and schedule an appointment?"

The best time to use this closing technique is when the prospect already seems sold on making the purchase. The main drawback of this method is that if the prospect says no, there's little you can do to turn the situation around.

2. *Assuming the prospect will place the order.*   Instead of asking if the prospect is interested in buying, this approach *assumes* that the sale already has been made:
- "If you'll just fill in this information, I'll finish writing up your order."
- "I agree with you that these are beautiful. They'll look perfect in your living room."

This closing technique is particularly successful when the prospect wants to buy but is reluctant to make the decision to go ahead. Since you have, in effect, made the decision for the prospect, there's no further obstacle. Beware, though, in using this technique—if you put too much pressure on the prospect, you can cause the sale to fall through.

3. *Giving the prospect a choice.* In this method of closing, the seller asks the prospect to choose one of two or more alternatives:

- "Do you prefer the blue or the green?"
- "Would you rather schedule your beauty treatment for Monday or Tuesday?"

The advantage of closing with a choice is that this makes it much easier for you to avoid a no answer. And by choosing one alternative over another, the prospect is essentially closing the sale for you.

4. *Providing an added inducement to buy.* This closing technique sweetens the pot by offering the prospect an added inducement (price discount, early delivery, extra service, and so on) to buy your product or service:

- "If you agree to place your order today, I'll pay for the shipping charges."
- "If you join today, you'll save $50 on your membership fee."

The added-inducement close may indeed result in a sale, but it lowers your profit, so you should use it sparingly.

5. *Warning the prospect to buy before it's too late.* This approach to closing can best be described as the don't-miss-the-boat strategy. By warning the prospect to buy before it is too late, the seller adds a sense of urgency to the purchase:

- "That's a limited edition print. To guarantee that the company has it in stock, I need to receive your order today."
- "Our new catalog comes out next week. I recommend that you place your order now while we know that the item is still available."

Although this technique is quite often successful, you should limit its use to those times when the product or service you are selling is in short supply. Otherwise you run the risk of developing a reputation for using high-pressure tactics.

SALES POINTERS

The suggestions that follow will help you to communicate more effectively with potential customers and strengthen your ability to make the sale.

1. *Sell the customer on you.*   Before you can sell people on the products or services you represent, you must first sell them on you. Since people are more inclined to buy from someone they trust and respect, your words, actions, and appearance must all combine to create the type of professional image that your customers expect. Network marketing is a distinctly personal business and *you* are the business, so your role is doubly important. To achieve your sales goals, you must work at building a positive rapport with each new prospect.

2. *Remember that the communication process is two-sided.* In addition to being a good speaker, you must also be a good listener. Don't get so caught up in the messages you are sending that you ignore the messages coming back. It's up to you to interpret the feedback that is generated and to respond accordingly.

3. *Put yourself in the customer's place.*   Good communicators know the importance of empathy—being able to see a situation from the other person's point of view. To communicate more effectively, instead of thinking why *you* like a product or how *you* would use it, try to think how it would benefit the prospect.

4. *Adapt your sales style to the customer.* People process information in different ways. Some people respond better to information they hear. Others respond to information they see or can touch. Keeping these differences in mind, you want to be sensitive to them and utilize the communication tools—words, visuals, hands-on demonstrations, and so on—that will get the best results.

5. *Ask questions.* To obtain a thorough understanding of the prospect's situation and needs, you must ask questions. Known as "probing," this technique entails getting the potential customer to open up and reveal the types of information you need in order to make the sale. In addition to helping you to sell more, probing can help you to develop a better relationship with your customers.

6. *Think before you speak.* During presentations, avoid the urge to "shoot from the lip." Rather than firing back to a question with the first answer that pops into your head, pause a moment to decide on the most appropriate response. The second or so you take to formulate your answer won't be noticed by the prospect, but the difference it makes in your answer will.

7. *Be enthusiastic.* If you aren't enthusiastic about what you sell through your network marketing business, why should the customer be interested? During your sales presentations, it's important to let customers know that you enjoy representing the MLM company you've chosen and are eager to show them how its products and services can benefit them.

8. *Be prepared.* In order to communicate well, you must have something to say. By planning your sales presentations ahead of time and mapping out the points

you want to cover and the visual aids you want to use, you'll be able to make effective use of your time with prospects.

9. *Believe in the product.*   You should only sell products that you believe in and that you feel are right for the prospect's needs. Top network marketers are not only motivated by making the sale, but by serving the best interests of their customers.

10. *Ask for the order.*   Whether you view an MLM presentation as "sharing," as some network marketers call it, or selling, the end result is the same. To be successful, ultimately you have to ask for the order. Many people are so afraid of rejection that they never ask. Although this eliminates the number of "no" responses they get, it also eliminates the "yes" responses, as well. So, take the initiative and *ask.*

6

Satisfying the Customer

The selling process doesn't stop when the sale is made—your real challenge is to keep the customer. This challenge is especially true for network marketers, since the people who are your best customers often turn out to be the best prospects to join your sales network. Thus, your number one priority should be satisfying your customers.

Considering the time and money needed to develop prospects and convince them to buy, it makes sense to maintain good customer relations. After all, it's easier to sell to a customer who's already sold on your business than it is to sell to someone who doesn't know anything about you. This explains many businesspeople's claims that "After the sale, we don't forget the service."

CUSTOMER SATISFIERS

As you can see in the diagram shown below, there are four elements that contribute to a customer's level of satisfaction.

The Product

The product or services you sell through your network marketing business must be appropriate for the customer's needs in terms of such key factors as purpose, quality, design, styling, durability, color, materials, and cost. No amount of salesmanship, personal attention, or promotion can overcome a defective or ill-conceived product. In the final analysis, the product must be able to perform up to the customer's expectations.

CUSTOMER SATISFIERS

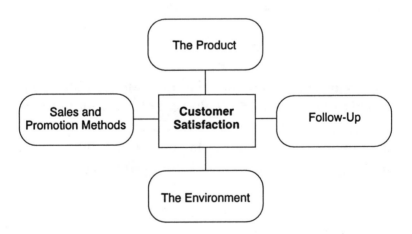

The Environment

The environment itself—the economy, trends of society, technology, political and legal forces—is a strong determinant of customer satisfaction, too. The products that are in demand and deliver satisfaction are those that are right for the times and the circumstances in which we live. For example, as the number of working women increases, the demand for labor-saving products and services (prepared foods, home shopping) goes up.

Sales and Promotion Methods

The sales and promotion methods that you use to contact the customer and to present your products can either add to or detract from the customer's satisfaction level. It is important to be aware of such things as the expectations you create, the way you treat each customer, and the type of impression you make. Overstating what a product can do is one of the surest ways to invite customer dissatisfaction. Demonstrating your product with knowledge and concern for the customer as an individual, on the other hand, will greatly enhance the customer's satisfaction level.

Follow-Up

Follow-up—the post-sales activities you perform to ensure that the customer gets what he or she bought—is crucial to creating customer satisfaction. As detailed in this chapter, follow-up consists of all the things you do to show your commitment to serving the customer's needs and to maintaining good customer relations.

THE NETWORK MARKETER AS MATCHMAKER

To achieve your goal of satisfying the customer, it helps to think of yourself as a matchmaker, matching your products or services with the needs of the customer. The more skillfully you are able to make the match, the more profitable your business will be on both a short-term and a long-term basis. The results of good matching are (1) satisfied customers, (2) continued patronage, and (3) customer referrals.

Satisfied Customers

You should make a distinction between satisfying your customers and selling to them. Since you get paid in both instances, the difference might not seem important, but it is. Many network marketing businesses start out strong, rapidly showing a profit and steadily increasing their sales volume. Then, seemingly without warning, things start to go wrong. Sales drop and loyal customers suddenly aren't interested in buying anymore. Why? What causes this to happen? It happens because the businesses were not really trying to meet the needs of their customers. They were more interested in "moving the goods" or "pushing services"—whether or not customers really needed them.

On a short-term basis, a strategy that emphasizes selling

over satisfying might seem like the way to go. It's quicker and easier, and the results can be readily seen on an income statement—for a while. On a long-term basis, though, satisfying your customer is what counts the most. Building a reputation for quality and service is what ultimately will enable you to *stay* in business.

Continued Patronage

The lifeblood of any business is the continued patronage of its customers. In addition to making the sale, you want to keep the customer coming back for more. When you develop a loyal following of customers who regularly buy from you, you have what is known as a *customer franchise*. This franchise can be one of your most valuable business assets since it represents virtually a presold market for your products and services. There is particular value in a customer franchise: when a business is sold, its purchase price is usually determined by the number of customers who regularly patronize it. The higher the number of active customer accounts that a business has, the higher the purchase price.

Customer Referrals

Building a loyal following of customers for your network marketing business means not only increased sales but increased customer referrals as well. When customers are pleased with the products or services they receive, it's only natural that they want to recommend them to others. These positive word-of-mouth referrals can cause your customer accounts to expand at an accelerated rate. For example, take a look at what happens when each of ten satisfied customers recommends your service to two other people who, in turn, tell two others who tell two more.

10	Satisfied customers
× 2	Others (friends, relatives, colleagues)
20	New prospects
× 2	Others
40	New Prospects
× 2	Others
80	New prospects

10 + 20 + 40 + 80 = 150 Total prospects

What started out as ten satisfied customers has mushroomed into a group of potential customers fifteen times that size—with a potential for even more growth.

In addition to illustrating the importance of positive word-of-mouth communication, this mushroom effect should also serve as a warning not to do anything to alienate your customers. *Negative* word-of-mouth comments travel just as far and as fast and can have a devastating effect on a business. The best way to guard against them is to maintain good customer relations.

MAINTAINING GOOD CUSTOMER RELATIONS

Maintaining good customer relations consists in helping customers to get the full benefits from their purchases. Beyond delivering what the customer paid for, it involves providing that "something extra" that's often necessary to ensure that the customer's needs are fully satisfied. Although each network marketing business is different, the most common methods for maintaining good customer relations include: (1) expediting the purchase, (2) providing personal service, (3) answering questions, (4) handling complaints, (5) solving problems, and (6) staying in touch with customers.

Expediting the Purchase

Once the customer has agreed to buy your product or service, the focus of your energy should shift from making the sale to completing the transaction. This means doing everything possible to expedite the purchase by (1) reassuring the customer that the purchase is the right one, (2) speeding delivery of the goods, and (3) overseeing any installation or implementation that may be required.

Something as simple as telling the customer "You'll get a lot of use out of that" or "You made a wise decision" can go a long way toward relieving any anxiety associated with the purchase. So can making sure that there are no delays in getting your product into the customer's hands or in performing the service that the customer expects. Nothing is more frustrating for a customer than deciding to buy something and then having to wait longer than necessary for the seller to deliver it. In conjunction with this, if your business is supposed to install or implement the product (computer equipment, a water purifier, a security system), it's your responsibility to see that the job is done correctly.

Providing Personal Service

Personal service may, in fact, be the best customer-relations tool that network marketers can utilize. With the growth of huge conglomerates, chains, and self-service outlets, personal service has become an endangered species. Customers who want to be treated as individuals are more likely to receive "cookie cutter" service that treats all customers the same. If you're able to provide the kind of personal service that is lacking elsewhere, you will have an edge over mass-produced customer service. The increasing number of bed-and-breakfast inns located throughout the United States provides a prime example of customer desires for personal attention. Rather than patronizing a hotel or motel, many travelers are choosing to stay at bed-and-breakfast inns. In place of color television sets, they are finding uniquely furnished rooms, home-cooked meals, and attentive innkeepers eager to make their stay memorable.

Regardless of your type of business, you can make it better by providing customers with personal service. For example, you can address each customer by name, take individual preferences into consideration, provide choices whenever possible, offer in-home or in-office shopping to accommodate busy schedules, provide special handling of rush deliveries, and, in general, do more than is expected. Since these "little things" often mean a lot to customers, paying attention to them puts your network marketing business at a distinct advantage over those businesses that ignore them.

Answering Questions

Being available to answer questions after the purchase has been made is essential for customer relations. It gives customers a sense of security to know that if they need additional information or instructions, they can always call you. This accessibility adds to the customer's satisfaction and helps keep minor problems or misunderstandings from becoming big ones. And by keeping the lines of communication open, you stand a better chance of making more sales in the future. Thus, instead of avoiding customers' questions or viewing them as time wasters, think of them as new opportunities to sell customers on your business and what it has to offer.

Handling Complaints

Part of your customer-relations effort, by necessity, must be directed at handling complaints. Just as customers can be expected to voice objections during sales presentations, they can also be expected to voice complaints after the sale is completed. Complaints are a fact of business life. The issue isn't really who's right or who's wrong but what needs to be done to satisfy the customer. Whenever a customer raises a complaint, your first concern should be to get to the heart of the problem as quickly as possible. If there is something wrong with your products or services, you want to determine what you can do to improve them. If a customer is unhappy with a purchase, you must decide how you can remedy the situation. Whatever the reason for a complaint, your sincere effort to resolve it will enhance the reputation of your business and result in additional positive word-of-mouth communications.

To handle complaints more efficiently and to let your customers know that you're on their side, it helps to follow these guidelines:

1. Listen to what the customer is telling you without interrupting.
2. Don't become defensive or angry.
3. Ask questions to get additional details, if necessary.
4. Show the customer that you care.
5. Take steps to resolve the problem as quickly as possible.
6. Thank the customer for bringing the problem to your attention.

Remember, there's a more difficult situation than having to deal with a dissatisfied customer who complains. The toughest situation of all is dealing with a dissatisfied customer who *doesn't* complain and just takes his or her business someplace else.

Solving Problems

The most successful sellers are problem solvers. After they make a sale, they go out of their way to help their customers put the products or services to best use. If a problem comes up, instead of saying "That's your problem," successful network marketers are willing to work with their customers to find a solution. When you do these things, you let customers know that you're on their side and are ready to use your expertise to help solve any problems they are experiencing.

Staying in Touch with Customers

Network marketers can also bolster their customer relations by staying in touch with customers on a regular basis. Instead of waiting for customers to contact you, take the initiative. You might telephone from time to time to see how customers are doing, send a card or a small gift to each customer at the Christmas–New Year season, or send out a mailing to provide customers with up-to-date information about your products or services. And, of course, when you make a new sale, it never hurts to send the customer a thank-you note.

To strengthen your ability to stay in touch with customers, you should maintain a file on each customer (individual or business) you serve. A sample file for individual customers is shown on page 106 and a file for business customers on page 107.

The better your filing system, the easier it will be for you to anticipate each customer's needs and to provide a high level of customer service.

RATING YOUR CUSTOMER RELATIONS

To make sure that you are doing everything possible to satisfy your customers, use the Customer Relations Evaluation Form on page 108 to rate yourself.

CUSTOMER FILE ENTRY	*Personal Data* Name of Spouse: —————— Name(s) of Children: —————— Special Interests: —————— Activities: —————— Other: ——————

Customer's Name: ————————————————

Street Address: ————————————————

City: ———————————— State: ——— Zip: ———

Telephone: (Home) ————— (Work) —————

Products/Services Currently Used: ——————

————————————————————————

————————————————————————

Personal Contact History

Date	Phone/ In Person	Purchases/Comments

BUSINESS FILE

CUSTOMER FILE ENTRY

Buyer's Name: ——————————

Title: ——————————

Personal Data:

Name of Spouse: ——————————

Name(s) of Children: ——————————

Interests/Hobbies: ——————————

Business Name: ——————————

Street Address: ——————————

City: —————————— State: ——— Zip: ———

Telephone: —————————— FAX: ——————

Type of Business: ——————————

Credit Rating: —————————— Usual Terms: ————

Products/Services Currently Used: ——————————

——————————

——————————

Personal Contact History

Date	Phone/ In Person	Purchases/Comments

CUSTOMER RELATIONS EVALUATION FORM

		Answer Yes or No
1.	My selling strategy is oriented toward satisfying each customer.	_____
2.	I work hard to encourage the continued patronage of customers rather than to just get the sale.	_____
3.	My goal is to establish lor.g-term customer relationships.	_____
4.	I try to get to know each customer as an individual, not just as an account.	_____
5.	I address each customer by name.	_____
6.	I always provide personal service.	_____
7.	When a customer has a question, I try to answer it as quickly as possible.	_____
8.	I handle complaints courteously and efficiently.	_____
9.	I am willing to work with the customer to solve any problems that arise.	_____
10.	I make sure that the customer receives the most prompt delivery or service possible.	_____
11.	I spend time reassuring the customer.	_____
12.	I give each customer something extra, not just the bare minimum.	_____
13.	I make a point of staying in touch with customers.	_____
14.	I believe the customer is always right.	_____

7

Building Your Network

Once you've launched the sales side of your business, you're ready to start building your network. As you move into this phase, the key to success is knowledge. The more you know about the MLM company you represent and its products and services, the more successful your recruitment and training efforts will be.

FINDING THE BEST PEOPLE

The people you will want to join your network should be people who will really make a contribution to the group, not just serve as names to fill in the spaces on your organization chart. The commitment of your recruits to the MLM sales program is more important than the actual number of people involved. The people you sponsor must be achievement-oriented individuals who possess the interpersonal skills and discipline necessary to succeed as network marketers.

In deciding whether or not a person would make the best recruit, look for these characteristics:

- Self-starting
- Desires to be successful
- Wants to make money
- Willing to work hard
- Enjoys working with people
- Communicates well
- Can lead and motivate
- Organized
- Goal-oriented
- Gets things done

It is not necessary for the people you recruit to have previous sales experience, although that would certainly be a plus. Nor is it necessary for them to have even worked before. Students and homemakers, for instance, may be new to the workforce but possess the very characteristics you're seeking.

There is no one type of person, in terms of age, occupation, education, or sex, who is more suited for network marketing than another. Network marketers come from all walks of life and represent all segments of the adult population. While a salesperson or someone with previous network marketing experience might be an ideal recruit, so might a teacher or an engineer. The teacher's classroom experience would certainly come in handy for giving presentations and conducting training sessions. The engineer, on the other hand, is likely to be organized and goal-oriented. People who take an active role in organizations or do volunteer work could be good prospects, too, given the contacts they have and their willingness to get involved. The same goes for people who participate in athletics (especially team sports like softball or soccer) since they have a competitive spirit and often know other like-minded people.

As a starting point for your recruitment activities, you would be wise to follow the advice of experienced network marketers: "Recruit your best customers." After all, who's more qualified to sell your company's products than someone who's already using them? Next, look to the people you know (family, friends, co-workers) and branch out from there through referrals and research to add to your leads. Using the same methods that you use to identify prospective customers (in Chapter 4), you can focus on those people who appear to have the "right stuff" to succeed in network marketing.

MAKING CONTACT

As soon as you've decided on the people you want to contact about joining your network, you can approach them in a number of ways: in person, by telephone, or by letter. More often than not, your goal during this initial contact will not be to discuss all the details about the MLM company you represent, but rather to make an appointment for the prospect to hear a business presentation.

The telephone tips that follow and the sample dialogue and letter should help you get started.

Telephone Tips

• Set success goals for yourself. Decide in advance how many appointments you want to make during each calling session. Then keep calling until you've reached your goal.

- Prepare a list of the people you want to call.
- Clear the work area around the telephone and have the materials (pen, paper, a calendar, and so on) you'll need within reach.
- Smile before you dial. Even though the prospect can't see you, your smile will come through in your voice.
- Get to the point of your call as quickly as possible— within the first three minutes. This not only heightens the impact of what you have to say, but shows respect for the prospect's time.
- Maintain a positive attitude. Just because one person says no does not mean that the next one will. As you become more experienced at singling out ("qualifying") your best prospects, you'll see the yes responses go up.
- Don't take rejection personally. Learn to deal with it and move on to your next prospect.
- Keep a record of each call that you make and its outcome.
- Enter all appointments in your calendar immediately. This will help to ensure that mixups don't occur.
- Don't book appointments more than a week in advance, if you can avoid it. This will make it easier to sustain the enthusiasm you generate during your initial contact.

Opening Dialogue

Face to Face

"_____, I've been meaning to tell you about this new business of mine (name of business). With your background in _____, I think it would be a perfect opportunity for you, too. When would be the best time for us to get together again this week so I can explain it to you?"

By Telephone

• *Family and Friends*

"Hello, _____. This is _____. I'm calling to tell you about this wonderful business opportunity I've gotten involved in recently. I know you've been interested in going into business for yourself and I think this might be just what you're looking for. When would be the best time this week for us to get together to discuss it?"

• *Acquaintances*

"Hello, _____. This is _____. We met last month at the (name of organization) meeting. I remembered that you had mentioned that you were interested in getting involved in a sideline business. Well, I think I have just the thing you're looking for. When would be the best time this week for us to get together to discuss it?"

• *Referrals*

"Hello, (Mr./Ms.) _____. This is _____. I'm calling you at the suggestion of _____. Do you have a minute to speak now or would you rather I called back at a more convenient time? I'm involved in a wonderful new business (name of business) and when I told _____ about it he/she thought you might be interested in it, too. I can send you some literature on it, or, if you prefer, we could get together later in the week to discuss it."

By Letter

Date

Name
Street Address
City, State   Zip Code

Dear _____:
I've recently gotten involved in a wonderful business
opportunity that I thought might be of interest to you. Since
I last saw you, I've become a representative for (name of
company).

Given your (background/interest) in _____, I wanted
to let you know about the company's marketing program
and invite you to attend a business presentation explaining
how it works.

Once you've had a chance to look over the enclosed
materials, I'll give you a call to discuss them. I'm looking
forward to seeing you again and to telling you more about
(name of company).

Sincerely,

Brad Stevens
Independent Representative

THE BUSINESS PRESENTATION

The business presentation to which you invite the
prospect can be (1) a presentation you put on yourself
or (2) a company-sponsored opportunity meeting.

Each method, as you can see, has its advantages and
disadvantages. You should use the method with which
you feel most comfortable and the one you think is
right for the prospect. Along with this, the MLM com-

PRESENTATION METHODS

Your Own Business Presentation

Advantages	Disadvantages
• More immediate • Personal • Can be tailored to prospect's interests • Can vary length of presentation	• Must prepare a presentation • Incomplete knowledge • May be unable to answer all questions • No back-up support from other representatives

Company-Sponsored Opportunity Meetings

Advantages	Disadvantages
• An experienced presenter • Professional environment • Audio/visual aids • Build excitement • Prospect can see other people joining	• No control over how information is presented • Impersonal • Good seating not always available • No guarantee prospect will attend • Prospect can see other people leaving

pany you represent will also be a key determinant in your method selection.

Some companies leave it up to representatives to do most of the presenting themselves. Conversely, other MLM companies host frequent, often elaborate, opportunity meetings and prefer to have representatives let company spokespersons tell the company's story and showcase the business plan. In this case, they advise representatives to use their contact time to "sell the meeting, not the business."

Holding Your Own Presentations

If you decide to hold your own business presentations for individuals or groups, then you will want to follow the same guidelines you use in planning and conducting your sales presentations. You need to find the best way to communicate the benefits associated with joining your network, to appeal to prospects' needs, and to be prepared to handle objections.

In the beginning, when you're just starting out, you're probably better off to limit your presentations to no more than a few people at a time. Then, after you've gained more experience and feel confident of your ability to work with a larger group, you can increase the meeting size, if you choose.

To help ensure that your presentations are as productive as they should be, try following these suggestions:

1. Greet each guest warmly and graciously and thank them for coming.
2. Give people a chance to get settled before you begin your presentation. Having ice water available or coffee and cookies is a good idea.
3. Look and act the part that is expected of you. Whether this calls for standard business attire or more casual clothing will depend on the product or service you sell.
4. Have everything you need for your presentation— brochures, presentation easel and charts, audio/ video equipment, and so on—in place before people arrive. Once your presentation is under way, you don't want to be looking for an extension cord or fumbling with a videotape.

5. Know your presentation format ahead of time so you are sure to make all your important points.

6. Pace yourself so your time is well used. Spending too much time on introductions may mean that you don't have enough time for a strong close at the end.

7. Provide the basic information people will need to make a decision about the business opportunity; include information on your product, company, compensation plan, multilevel marketing concept, and the method for becoming a network member.

8. Be enthusiastic. Explain why you think the business opportunity is such a good one and the difference it can make in people's lives if they decide to get involved.

9. Ask prospects to join your network. Have representative forms and order blanks close at hand so that you can complete the paperwork without delay if they are ready to join.

10. Conclude the presentation on an upbeat note, thanking everyone for their time and making arrangements to meet with your new distributors as soon as possible to help all interested people get started in the program.

Utilizing Company-Sponsored Opportunity Meetings

If you're going to invite prospects to attend company-sponsored opportunity meetings, you should make it a point to first attend one or more meetings yourself so you know how they are run. Being familiar with the foremat, content, and location of the meeting will not only make it easier for you to answer prospects' questions (How long is the meeting? where is it? where should I park? and so forth), but will enable you to better utilize the meeting.

To get the most out of opportunity meetings, be sure to:

1. Call prospects prior to the meeting to confirm that they are going to attend and to make sure that they have the correct details: date, time, location.
2. Plan to arrive early for the meeting so that you can take care of the registration procedures and assure yourself of getting good seats for you and your guests.
3. Introduce your guests to your sponsor or other members of your network who are at the meeting. This will help the people you've invited to feel more involved in the proceedings and will give you an opportunity to tell them about the success the others are having with the company's program.
4. Pay attention during the meeting so that you can answer prospects' questions later.
5. Be enthusiastic. Even if you know the presenter's talk by heart, be sure not to appear bored or disinterested.
6. Have your sales materials ready, but don't show them to prospects until after the meeting.
7. Know ahead of time what you want to do after the presentation is over. You should know not only *what* to say, but also *where* to say it. For example, you may want to turn your chair to face the prospect or, if the room is crowded, move to a quieter location—

a corner of the room, the hotel lobby, or a coffee shop.

8. Ask the prospect to join your network. If the presentation has already sold the prospect on the business opportunity, you can go ahead and complete the sign-up process at this time. Conversely, if the prospect still isn't convinced, you can answer questions or handle any objections that are raised.

9. Make arrangements to meet with new representatives as soon as possible to help them get started with the program.

10. Give uncommitted prospects a brochure, a copy of the company's marketing plan, or other materials to take home with them. Then plan a follow-up in a few days to discuss the program with them again.

PROVIDING TRAINING AND SUPPORT

The best network marketers not only recruit well, but they train well. If you want your network to grow, you must be prepared to offer new recruits the training and support they need to succeed. This means helping representatives to set goals for themselves, showing them how to get started, suggesting ways to develop their business skills, and simply being available to answer questions or give encouragement.

Whenever you add new members to your network, make it a point to do the following:

• Provide them with company training and marketing materials.

- Review the company's policies and procedures.
- Familiarize them with the company's products and services.
- Explain how to fill out the forms they will be using and provide samples they can follow.
- Help them to identify their target markets and come up with leads to contact.
- Offer suggestions on the best ways to approach prospective customers.
- Invite them to sit in on your sales presentations so they can gain first-hand experience in selling.
- Emphasize the importance of setting realistic goals.
- Inform them of the times and locations of company-sponsored opportunity meetings.
- Show them how to get in touch with other members, including *your* sponsor.
- Help them to build their own networks.

In addition to working with new representatives in this way, you should plan to provide ongoing training and support for *all* network members in your group. Calling members from time to time to say hello or to share information shows your concern. Holding periodic meetings during the year to discuss topics of interest, such as sales techniques, ways to generate leads, promotion strategies, time management, record keeping, and so on, also helps create a stimulating and informative work environment for your representatives. Organizing occasional social events, too, can go a long way toward building morale and team spirit. Rather than feeling alone or isolated, representatives can interact with each other at a picnic, potluck dinner, or other event and share in one another's success.

8

Managing Your Time

One thing all network marketers have in common, regardless of the products or services they sell, is the need to make good use of their time. Multilevel marketing is a labor-intensive business in which your primary resource is time—*your* time. In order to accomplish what needs to be done and to achieve your goals, you must become adept at time management.

TIME—AN ACCOUNTABLE ASSET

To improve your time-management skills, start by asking yourself the all-important question, "Where does my time go?" Surprisingly enough, many people who can easily account for the money they spend often find themselves at a loss when it comes to accounting for their time. This is especially true of network marketers who work at home or who are involved in more than one business enterprise. Given the need to juggle several activities at once, which often occurs in this situation, it's easy to lose track of the time spent on any one activity or task.

Keeping a Time Log

The simplest way to find out where your time goes is to keep a daily record, or *time log*, detailing how you spend each waking hour in the day. By filling in a log similar to the one shown on page 123, you can easily determine the amount of time you spend on each activity.

After a week or so of accounting for your time in this way, you should go over the logs and ask yourself these questions:

1. What activities took up the greatest amount of my time?
    *   How important were those activities?
    *   Could I have done the activities in less time?
    *   Could I have eliminated any activities? If so, how?
2. What things happened over which I had no control?
    *   Could I have handled those situations better?
3. What were my biggest time wasters?
4. What percentage of my time did I really spend productively?
5. Did I accomplish the things I set out to do?
6. How could I use my time more effectively?

No doubt you will discover that time frequently does not go where it's supposed to go or where you think it has gone. For instance, the "five-minute" phone conversation you had with a new network member actually

DAILY TIME LOG

Date _____

How I Spent My Time

7:00 _____   3:00 _____

_____   _____

_____   _____

8:00 _____   4:00 _____

_____   _____

_____   _____

9:00 _____   5:00 _____

_____   _____

_____   _____

10:00 _____   6:00 _____

_____   _____

_____   _____

11:00 _____   7:00 _____

_____   _____

_____   _____

12:00 _____   8:00 _____

_____   _____

_____   _____

1:00 _____   9:00 _____

_____   _____

_____   _____

2:00 _____   10:00 _____

_____   _____

_____   _____

lasted twenty minutes. The "minute or so" that it takes to order more inventory turns out to be closer to an hour. Everyday interruptions, unforeseen occurrences, and emergencies have a way of eating into one's time, too. Added to this is the tendency of entrepreneurs in general to set unrealistic goals for themselves, fully expecting to accomplish two days' work in one day's time.

Armed with the information in your daily time logs, you can approach the issue of time from a realistic perspective. Rather than focusing on how you "think" you spend your time or "would like to" spend your time, you can focus on how you *actually* spend it.

OVERCOMING TIME WASTERS

One of the first things to look for in reviewing your time logs is time wasters—activities that took up your time but were ultimately unproductive. Examples include having your telephone call placed on hold, redoing paperwork that you filled out incorrectly, waiting for a prospective network member who's late for a business presentation, or looking for a misplaced file. Taken individually—a minute here and a few minutes there— each activity doesn't amount to much. But when totalled, time wasters can actually eclipse the time you spend productively.

A time waster may be internally generated by you or externally generated by others or events. An inadequate filing system that causes you to spend too much time looking for things is an *internal* time waster—you control it. On the other hand, waiting for your telephone call to be taken is an *external* time waster—you have no control over it.

Internally generated time wasters are the easiest to eliminate because they are the result of your own actions. Once these actions are changed, the time waster disappears. Externally generated time wasters pose more of a problem. Since these time wasters are beyond your control, you can't totally eliminate them and must sometimes simply make the best of them; for example, while you're on hold you can do your paperwork, draw up a list, or review notes for a presentation.

The first step toward eliminating or dealing with time wasters is to identify them. The following chart shows some of the most common ones.

TIME WASTERS

Internal	External
___ Unorganized desk	___ Telephone interruptions
___ Inadequate filing system	
	___ Waiting for people
___ Inefficient work layout	___ Stuck in traffic
___ Poor scheduling	___ Lack of information
___ Procrastination	___ Excessive paperwork
___ Lack of priorities	___ Misunderstandings
___ Insufficient planning	___ Equipment breakdowns
___ Failure to communicate	
	___ Neighbors' visits
___ Indecision	___ Incompetent people
___ Spreading yourself too thin	___ Unclear policies and procedures
___ Inability to say no	
_____	_____
_____	_____
_____	_____
_____	_____

Strategies for Overcoming Time Wasters

Having identified *your* time wasters, you can use these strategies to overcome them.

1. *Organize your work environment.* Papers, files, supplies, and equipment should all be in their own special places and readily accessible when you need them. Instead of continually wasting time looking for misplaced messages and files or walking extra steps to reach supplies and equipment, you must organize your work environment—now. If it means getting more filing cabinets or shelves, get them as soon as possible.

2. *Formulate objectives.* Formulating objectives for yourself and your business gives you something to shoot for—a direction to follow. Once your objectives are clear, procrastination and indecision should no longer be problems.

3. *Set priorities.* Instead of trying to do everything at once or spending too much time on unimportant activities, rank all your activities in order of importance. Then focus first on those activities that have the highest priority. Low priority items should be postponed until last, delegated to others when possible, or eliminated.

4. *Communicate clearly.* Just because something seems obvious to you doesn't mean it is obvious to others. Taking care to communicate clearly will save you time and money in the long run by reducing the number of time-wasting misunderstandings and mistakes that occur and the number of unnecessary phone calls and letters needed to clear up the misunderstandings and mistakes.

5. *Screen telephone calls.* If you are trying to meet a deadline or if you simply need some quiet time to

yourself, use a telephone answering service or machine to screen your calls. You can quickly return those calls requiring your immediate attention and put off returning the less important calls until a more convenient time. Even if you answer the phone yourself, don't be afraid to tell the caller if it is a bad time for you and get back to them later.

6. *Use remnant time.* Remnant time—the intervals between scheduled activities—is quite often wasted. It can be the half-hour gap between meetings or the 20 minutes spent waiting for a customer who's running late. Bit by bit, the remnant time adds up. Rather than wasting it, though, you can use it to take care of low-priority or routine activities. Returning a phone call, writing a letter, reviewing your notes for a presentation, or checking supplies are just some of the things that could be accomplished during remnant time.

7. *Keep equipment in good repair.* To avoid having equipment break down just at the moment you need it the most, establish a regular maintenance schedule for the equipment used in your business. As a further precaution, you should keep a list of numbers to call for emergency repairs or rental equipment.

8. *Learn your company's policies and procedures.* To keep things going smoothly, make sure that you understand your MLM company's policies and procedures. This will reduce misunderstandings and help you to avoid making mistakes when filling out paperwork or submitting information.

9. *Learn to say no.* The next time someone requests that you volunteer your services, stop and ask yourself a few questions: Is this something I really want to do? Would it be a good use of my time? Could someone else

just as easily do it? This approach cuts back not only on time wasters but also on the stress caused by taking on too many responsibilities.

10. *Act now.*   Probably the biggest time waster of all is procrastination—putting off till tomorrow what can be done today. Once you've made a decision to do something, begin to lay the groundwork for carrying it out. By acting immediately, rather than later, you have a better chance of actually accomplishing what you set out to do.

SETTING PRIORITIES

In setting priorities for the things you wish to accomplish, it helps to use a *daily planner* similar to the one shown on page 129. Consisting of a "things to do" list, priority chart, and schedule, the daily planner enables you to rank your activities in order of importance and to track the progress of each task through to completion. Activities that are not completed by the end of the day are carried over to the next day, the day after that, and so on until eventually they are either completed or eliminated.

The important thing to remember in organizing your time is that you should always give your attention to top-priority items first. Low-priority items can be tempting, especially when they are easier to do and take up less time, but it's a mistake to start with them. If you do, you may never finish the top- and high-priority tasks. So, instead of completing three low-priority items, you would do better to complete 20 percent of the work on one top-priority item.

Granted, setting priorities and sticking to them isn't

DAILY PLANNER

Date _____

Things to Do

_____

_____

_____

_____

_____

_____

_____

	Priorities	Comments/ Status
Top		
High		
Med.		
Low		

Schedule

7:00 _____

8:00 _____

9:00 _____

10:00 _____

11:00 _____

12:00 _____

1:00 _____

2:00 _____

3:00 _____

4:00 _____

5:00 _____

6:00 _____

7:00 _____

8:00 _____

9:00 _____

10:00 _____

easy. There will always be those days when everything cries out for your immediate attention and all of your projects should have been completed yesterday. But, as your time-management skills improve, the frustrating days will become fewer and farther between.

BALANCING BUSINESS AND FAMILY NEEDS

At times, meeting the needs of your business and your family will probably seem like a juggling act. No matter how well thought out a time schedule is, the unforeseen and urgent needs of family members can easily throw it out of balance. There will also be occasions when your family resents your network marketing business and its demands for your attention.

It is still possible, however, to have a successful business, enjoy your work, and *not* sacrifice your home life in the process. Along with time-management skills, you need an understanding of how family members feel about your network marketing business and the anxieties it might be causing them. You'll find it easier to balance business and family needs if you follow a few suggestions.

1. *Get your family involved in the business.* Family members will be more supportive of your network marketing activities if they feel a part of what's happening. Even if you don't need help or if family members are not willing to help, you can still get them involved in what you're doing by keeping them informed of your progress. New ideas, sales figures, successful presentations, the size of your network, and the goals you've set for yourself should be shared with them. Remember, it

will be easier for your family to care if you take the time to share.

2. *Make it a learning experience.*   If you have children at home, try to make the business a learning experience for them. Depending on their ages and interests, your children may be able to help out in a number of ways, including unpacking product deliveries, putting away supplies and arranging merchandise, taking messages, and helping you to prepare for presentations. One network marketer said that her young son got so involved in the business that he wanted her to teach him how to do the sales demos so *he* could sell the merchandise.

If you do get your children to help with the business, for the best results, you should (1) explain to them that their work is important, (2) reward them for their time, and (3) make the business fun for them. Obviously your goal is not to get free labor but to broaden your children's realm of experiences and to let them be a part of what you're doing.

3. *Develop a support network.*   A support network consisting of baby-sitters, housekeepers, friends, and others who can lend a hand when needed can also help you to juggle your time. Help of this sort is especially important if you're taking care of small children whose needs for attention are more or less constant.

4. *Set aside time for your family.*   Schedule specific times to spend with your family, and let them know that during these times they will have your undivided attention. Whatever you decide to do, whether you plan something special or just have a meal together and talk, the needs of the business will not be allowed to intrude on your family time.

5. *Don't be too critical of yourself.*   Accept the fact that things will not always go as planned, and learn to live with that. Sometimes you won't get as much work done as you had hoped; other times you'll feel selfish for not devoting more time to your family. These conflicts are to be expected and are part of the price you pay for being an entrepreneur. It's important to recognize that you can't always be all things to all people or operate at a 100 percent efficiency level. So make allowances when necessary. After all, you're only human.

TIME-MANAGEMENT TIPS

The following suggestions should help you to make the best use of your time.

1. Find out where your time goes by using a daily time log to keep track of how each hour is spent.
2. Identify time wasters and develop strategies for overcoming them.
3. Set realistic daily goals for yourself.
4. Use a daily planner to help organize what needs to be done and to schedule your time.
5. Reserve your most productive times during the day for the top- and high-priority items on your "things to do" list.
6. Take shortcuts whenever possible; for instance, a phone call is quicker than a letter.
7. Learn to simplify and standardize tasks and to eliminate the ones that are unnecessary.
8. Handle each piece of incoming mail one time only; that is, make a decision as you read it to (1) respond to it, (2) file it, or (3) throw it away.

9. Schedule "minibreaks" of ten to twenty minutes throughout the day to relax; then begin your work again, refreshed.

10. Fill out your daily planner each night so that in the morning you can start off with your first activity of the day.

9

Motivating Yourself and Your People

The best time-management system in the world will be of little use to you if you aren't motivated by the desire to succeed. To use your time well, you have to *want* to accomplish something. When your network marketing business is just getting started, motivation isn't likely to be a problem. The challenge of learning about the MLM company you represent, generating leads, and identifying potential network members should be motivation enough to keep you going. But once the initial excitement begins to wear off, the need for self-motivation becomes more important.

Without someone—commonly known as "the boss"— to give you direction and reward your efforts, it's up to you to motivate yourself. Your sponsor and other upline network members can provide advice and guidance, but ultimately you're the one responsible for taking the initiative to do the things that are necessary to succeed. This means coming up with new ways to keep your enthusiasm level high and to maintain the sense of satisfaction that you get from your business.

SETTING GOALS

One way to stay motivated is to set goals for yourself. Rather than thinking of success in abstract or unattainable terms, you can break it down into individual goals to be accomplished. For each goal, you should indicate your plan of action for achieving it and specify a target date for its completion. Then, as each date arrives, your *actual* performance can be compared with your *intended* performance.

Whenever a goal is reached, a new goal should be set. In this way, you can keep both your momentum and motivation going strong. For example, your goals for the first year of your network marketing business might look like this:

Months 1–2

- Read *Build Your Own Network Sales Business.*
- Set up network marketing business.
- Familiarize myself with company-provided marketing and training materials.
- Do market research.
- Identify potential customers and network members.
- Invite prospects to sales presentations and business opportunity meetings.

Months 3–5

- Generate $ _____ in sales commissions.
- Build my network to three levels.
- Begin conducting my own opportunity meetings.

Months 6–8

- Increase monthly sales by ___ percent.
- Add _____ new network members per month.

Months 9–10

- Help at least ____ network members a month to move up to the next level.

By End of Year 1

- Earn $ _____ annual income.
- Reach the _____ level in my organization.
- Win one of the company's Outstanding Achiever awards.

In order for the goal-setting process to work, the goals that you set for yourself should be:

1. *Measurable.* It isn't enough just to say that you want to "do well" or "be a success." There must be some criterion (sales volume, number of network members, your level in the organization, and so on) to indicate when a goal has been reached. Unless there is some standard of measurement that can be used to define, or "quantify," a goal that you've set for yourself, there's no way to know when you've satisfied it.

2. *Scheduled.* Each goal that you set for yourself should have a specific time frame for its completion. If

you have to move a date up or push it back, you can. But, having a completion date to shoot for will make it easier for you to schedule the work that needs to be done to accomplish the goal and to monitor your progress—Are you on schedule, behind schedule, or ahead of schedule?

3. *Realistic.*   Setting unrealistic goals for yourself is just setting yourself up for failure. Few people become "overnight" millionaires or earn enough to retire within six months of starting their businesses. Look at what others have accomplished in the MLM company you belong to and at how long it took them to do it. Then compare this to your own circumstances and set your goals accordingly. Keep in mind that the closer the goals for your business are to your own personal goals, the greater the likelihood that you will achieve them.

4. *In Writing.*   A goal that isn't in writing isn't a goal, as management experts will tell you. By writing down the things you want to accomplish, you help them to become real. Putting your goals in writing not only clarifies them, but makes it easier to keep them in focus as you work toward attaining them.

Develop Action Plans

Goals are destinations you want to reach. Action plans are what get you there. For each goal that you set for yourself, you should also develop an action plan for achieving it. For example, if one of your goals is to increase your monthly sales by 25 percent, you should determine what steps you need to take to accomplish that, calculating:

- The number of hours per week you will need to work.
- The number of leads you will need to generate.
- The number of sales presentations you must give.
- The average dollar amount each sale must be.

The advantage of using action plans and the reason why they are such a necessary part of goal setting is that they tell you how to turn your goals into realities. With an action plan, you know the time, the work, and the people involved in getting where you want to go. Rather than striking out in all directions at once, getting discouraged, and losing your momentum, you can concentrate on the actions that are central to your success.

Stay Flexible

One of the reasons that people are often reluctant to set goals for themselves is that they are afraid of getting stuck—tied down to a plan of action that isn't right for them. This doesn't have to be the case, nor should it be.

To get the most value from the goal setting process, it's important to stay flexible. That way, if your needs change or the needs of your customers or network members change, you can modify your goals to reflect the new situation. By staying flexible, rather than sticking with a plan that isn't working, you'll be able to take advantage of new opportunities and keep yourself motivated.

So, *do* put your goals on paper and actively pursue them. But know that you can erase them later if you want to and substitute new goals that are more meaningful to you and that you are motivated to achieve.

Don't Go It Alone

Just as network marketing draws its strength from people power, so does goal setting. Contrary to what you might think, the majority of successful people do *not* go it alone. If you were to talk to most of them, they would tell you that they had help in achieving their goals.

To keep yourself motivated and to accomplish what you set out to do, seek out positive, achievement-oriented people with whom you can share ideas and information. By joining organizations and going to meetings and seminars where you can come into contact with successful people, you can learn first-hand what it takes to succeed.

Also remember that when you're working toward a major goal, it's important to *state your goals to someone you respect and admire.* The encouragement you are given will help to keep you going. What's more, by verbalizing the goal, you bring it out in the open and increase your level of commitment to it.

DEVELOPING ALL DIMENSIONS OF YOURSELF

To stay motivated and to build your network marketing business into the successful enterprise you want it to be, you must work at developing yourself into the person you want to be. This means recognizing yourself for the multidimensional human being that you are and developing all your dimensions: the physical, intellectual, emotional, and spiritual.

HUMAN DIMENSIONS

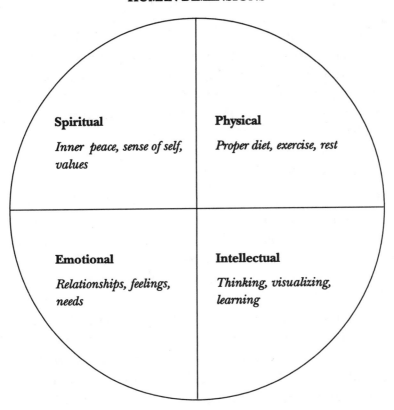

Your Physical Dimension

In order to succeed in network marketing, you must have the strength and energy it takes to carry out the day-to-day tasks of running your business. If you feel tired all the time or look worn out, you won't be able to do your best work or win the confidence of your customers and network members.

Eating the right foods, getting enough sleep, and

exercise all contribute to your physical well-being. Skipping meals or eating a steady diet of snacks and fast food is not to your long-term advantage. Neither is neglecting the need for exercise. The 30 minutes or so a day that it takes to walk, run, do aerobics, or exercise in some other way will be more than offset by your gain in stamina and productivity, not to mention improved health.

Following Your Body Clock

If you experience a decline in motivation and can't pinpoint the reason for it, it may be attributed to nothing more serious than trying to force your body to do something it doesn't want to do. In other words, you may be working against your body clock, rather than following it.

Each person's body has its own natural timing mechanism that dictates when the body has the most energy, hence the tendencies of some people to be "day people" and others to be "night people." Rather than trying to change your body clock, part of your development process should entail getting in touch with it and becoming aware of your high-energy times. These times can then be reserved for the most important items on your daily "things to do" list, thus enabling you to accomplish more and keep your motivation level up.

Your Intellectual Dimension

Just as your body requires exercise to stay strong and healthy, so does your mind. To fully reach your potential and keep yourself moving toward your goals, you must develop your intellectual capacities. This not only means making a conscious effort to sharpen your thinking and reasoning skills, but also to get past the psychological barriers ("I couldn't do that," "It's too difficult," "I don't have the time," and so on) that keep you from achieving all that you could.

The learning process needs to be an ongoing one, not something that ends when a person's school years are over. Rather than succumbing to the lure of the television set for hours on end, why not read a biography about someone who interests you? Or explore a new subject you've always wanted to know more about? You could attend a seminar or enroll in a class at your local community college. Listen to motivational tapes. Read some of the great works of literature. Do whatever appeals to you, as long as you keep your mind open to new inputs, hone skills you already have, and uncover new skills.

Your Emotional Dimension

There's a tendency among many people to deny their emotions, as if to acknowledge them would be a sign of weakness. By limiting themselves to looking at facts, not feelings, they develop their rational, deliberate dimension at the expense of their emotional dimension. As a result, they miss out on many of the joys life has to offer and on the opportunities to take pleasure from the things they have worked so hard to attain.

Your own personal success and the success of your network marketing business is dependent on your ability to enter into mutually-supportive relationships, to openly express your feelings, hopes, dreams, and fears to others, and to allow others to share with you as well. Communicating, encouraging, sharing each other's lives— these are things that will enrich you and keep you going. Allow your emotional dimension to put you in touch with the people you care about and to motivate yourself and others to overcome the obstacles that get in your way.

Your Spiritual Dimension

Your spiritual dimension is perhaps the hardest to understand since it is the most elusive. In a religious sense, it is one's belief in a greater force beyond oneself, in God. In a philosophical sense, it is one's purpose in life or, as the French philosophers called it, one's *raison d'être,* "reason for being."

However you view it, your spiritual dimension is one that you must not ignore. In it, you will find your sense of self—the person you really are—and the inner peace that comes from fulfilling your own promise.

To develop this side of yourself, you must learn to channel your own personal strength and values into positive thoughts and actions. This inner search means finding what you want to do in life and *doing* it—putting your talents and abilities to good use, rather than wasting them. You will have to look within yourself to discover your true nature and what's important to you. You will also have to look at the world around you and determine how you can contribute to making it a better place.

Along this line, you should work at "visualizing" your success and the person you want to be. By forming a mental image of yourself living the life you want to live, you can actually influence your behavior so that you begin "acting the part" and doing the things that will move you closer to your vision. It's important to note that the reverse is true as well. People who see themselves as failures are likely to become failures. So you want to build a positive mental image of yourself and to take every opportunity to reinforce it by focusing on your strengths and accomplishments.

When each of your four dimensions is strong and healthy and you feel empowered to meet the challenges that life presents you, you'll find that motivation comes naturally. If you enjoy what you're doing and are confident in your ability to achieve your goals, you'll create the impetus you need to move ahead.

MOTIVATION PRINCIPLES

To keep your motivation level up and to reinforce your commitment to accomplishing the things that are important to you, keep these principles in mind:

- Have a positive outlook.
- Believe in yourself.
- Maintain your self-esteem.
- Set meaningful goals for yourself.
- Develop action plans.
- Be persistent.
- Find ways to derive enjoyment from your work.
- Maintain your enthusiasm.
- Don't be overly critical of yourself.
- Don't worry about making mistakes.
- Avoid people who are negative.

- Develop all dimensions of yourself: physical, intellectual, emotional, and spiritual.
- Never stop learning.
- Ask for help when you need it.
- Visualize your success.
- See yourself as you want to be.
- Let others share in your success.
- Set new challenges for yourself.
- Savor your accomplishments.
- Be grateful for your good fortune.

MOTIVATING OTHERS

One of your primary responsibilities as a network marketer will be to develop ways to motivate the people in your network. Your motivation tactics will not be a substitute for the self-motivation that each network member must generate, but they can add significantly to that. Rather than signing up new members and then leaving them on their own to sink or swim, you must help them get started and guide them in developing their own networks. By letting the people you sponsor know that you believe in them, understand the challenges they face, and are there to help them achieve their goals, you can work wonders.

Being There

The most basic motivator of all is simply to let the members of your group know that you are there for them. Whether they've just made a big sale and want to share the good news with someone or they are feeling frustrated and need someone to encourage them, it's important for them to know you're "just a phone call away." When questions arise over how to fill out a form, the best way to make contact with a prospect, what presentation methods to use, time management, or whatever, they should know you're available to offer advice and information and, even more important, to provide something that the training manuals and video tapes cannot—your friendship and support.

Sharing Your Vision

In order to motivate the members of your network, you must share with them your vision of success and show them how your vision relates to their vision. And to share your vision, you must be able to put it into words and communicate it to others—this ability to share a vision of success and to convince others to commit to achieving success is one of the traits that mark a leader.

How can you put your vision into words? Try thinking of a confident you doing interesting, worthwhile work and helping others to do the same thing. Think not just of the income you want to make, but of how you would use the income to buy the material possessions, the freedom of action (traveling, enjoying cultural events), and the time to enhance the quality of your life and that of others (through charities and through relaxing with family and friends). The more concrete and believable you can make your vision, the more it will come alive for those with whom you want to share it. The closer your vision is to the one that your fellow network marketers want for themselves, the greater the likelihood that they will make the vision their own and incorporate it into their own vision of success.

Identifying Needs

Just as important as the ability to identify your customers' needs is the ability to identify your network members' needs. No one incentive works for all people. A goal that's important to one network member may not be to another. One person's top priority could easily be someone else's lowest priority. Whereas the main motivation for one network member might be money, for another member it might be a flexible work schedule or a chance for personal creativity.

To effectively motivate the people you sponsor, you must find out which of their needs are unfulfilled and determine the importance they place on each one. For instance, someone who is in debt or is barely making ends meet is obviously going to be more motivated by the money they can earn as an MLM company distributor than by the opportunity to make new friends. The very opposite could be true for someone who's new to your community and doesn't know very many people. A person with low self-esteem is likely to respond to praise. A high achiever, who's already doing well, might do even better if given the opportunity to serve as a role model to others.

The trick, of course, is to know the right motivational appeal to use. Through your personal observations and talks with network members, you should be able to gather enough information to discover which incentives will work best with which individuals.

Recognizing Accomplishments

Everyone likes to be noticed and rewarded for their accomplishments. One of the advantages of network marketing is that, with its different levels and bonuses, it is designed to offer many personal rewards. In addition to the recognition the MLM company provides, there are ways you, as a group leader, can recognize network members' accomplishments. Writing a note or phoning to congratulate a distributor who meets a key goal is one way to show your admiration. Taking the distributor out to lunch is another way to show your appreciation. On a broader scale, you could do what some successful network marketers do—give out a variety of regular monthly awards or prizes. The prizes might be for the highest sales total, the most new network members, the best attitude, the most creative presentations, and so on. The awards or prizes needn't be expensive—a certificate, a personalized T-shirt, a desk accessory, flowers—make simple and thoughtful gifts.

Making It Fun

Successful people often say that they think of their work as fun rather than as a chore. As a result, they end up working harder and becoming even more successful. Always remember to make it fun to be in your network!

If the people you sponsor enjoy being a part of your organization, they will work harder to meet both their own goals and the broader goals of the MLM company.

Contests, social events, guest speakers, and skits and demonstrations at meetings can all help to make the network marketing experience an enjoyable one for your members. Along with this, they can heighten the team spirit that members feel and add to their sense of belonging to the group.

10

Balancing the Books

As the owner of a network marketing business, you must keep good financial records—for the government *and* for yourself. The success of your business depends on careful record keeping. And the more accurate and up-to-date your records are, the easier it will be to prepare your income tax returns.

THE VALUE OF GOOD RECORDS

Setting up an efficient record-keeping system is the best way to ensure that you receive all of the business-related tax deductions to which you are entitled. Your records can also be a valuable tool in making business decisions and in helping you to identify problems and take corrective action. Good records enable you to substitute facts for guesswork, continuity for confusion. Instead of having to hunt for financial information or develop it on the spot, you already have it in hand, waiting to be used. For example, your record-keeping system should be able to provide you information on:

- Monthly sales totals
- Commissions earned
- Business operating expenses
- Amount of money invested in inventory
- Products or services most in demand
- Sales made on credit
- Identity of your best customers
- Financial obligations coming due
- Total value of your assets
- Overall profitability

And, in addition to depicting the financial history of your network marketing business, your records provide a scorecard you can use to rate its performance.

CHOOSING THE BEST SYSTEM

The Internal Revenue Service does not stipulate the kind of records a business owner must keep, only that the records properly identify the business's income, expenses, and deductions. Thus, you may use any record-keeping system that meets this criterion and is suited to your network marketing business. For best results, the system you choose should be (1) simple to use, (2) easy to understand, (3) accurate, (4) consistent, and (5) capable of providing timely information.

You can choose from among a number of business record-keeping systems, ranging from simple to complex. The simplest of these are the single-entry and pegboard systems, available at stationery and business-forms stores;

the most complex is the double-entry system, used by accountants.

Single-Entry Record-Keeping System

The single-entry record-keeping system is based on your income statement rather than your balance sheet. Thus, unlike the double-entry accounting system, it does not require you to "balance the books" or record more than one entry for each transaction. The simplicity of the system is its best feature and the one that makes it so appealing to the owners of new or small businesses. For tax purposes, the system enables you quickly and easily to record the flow of income and expenses generated by your business. In addition to this, a good single-entry record-keeping system provides a means of keeping track of your accounts receivable, accounts payable, depreciable assets, and inventory.

For help in setting up a single-entry record-keeping system specifically tailored to the needs of your network marketing business, consult an accountant or bookkeeper. Or you may find that one of the commercially available ready-made systems is sufficient for your needs. Generally consisting of worksheets bound together in a spiral notebook, these systems can be purchased for less than $15 at office-supply and stationery stores. The most popular single-entry system is the one put out by Dome Publishing Company.

Pegboard Record-Keeping System

The pegboard record-keeping system is actually a single-entry system since it requires only one entry per business transaction. But its design and the way you use it put it in a category by itself. For one thing, it is an all-in-one system that not only keeps track of your records but also provides materials for writing checks and issuing receipts. The system derives its name from the fact that the checks and receipts it uses are overlaid, one after another, on top of your permanent record sheets and held in place by pegs. Whenever you write a check or receipt, the information is automatically transferred, via carbon paper, to the record sheet below. This feature is particularly valuable because it eliminates the cause of the majority of record-keeping errors—forgetting to enter a transaction in the books.

The price of a pegboard system can range from $75 to $200, depending on the system's size and complexity. This includes the printing costs for personal checks and receipts. Consult the Yellow Pages under "Business Forms and Systems" for the pegboard-system specialists near you.

Double-Entry Record-Keeping System

The double-entry record-keeping system is more involved than the single-entry and pegboard systems. But because of its built-in checks and balances, this system provides greater accuracy and may be better suited to your business. Based on the balance sheet rather than the income statement, it requires that two entries be made for every recorded transaction. This double-entry concept is based on the fact that all business transactions involve an exchange of one thing for another. For instance, if a customer buys merchandise from you and pays cash for it, the amount of money in your business increases while at the same time the inventory level decreases. Under the double-entry system, you must record both changes in your books—one as a debit and the other as a credit. This is where the checks and balances come in: For each transaction, the total debit amount must always equal the total credit amount. If the amounts are out of balance, the transaction has been improperly recorded.

Unless you have had some bookkeeping or accounting experience, you will probably need help to set up and maintain a double-entry system. Many network marketers have a bookkeeper come in once a week or once a month, as needed, to do their books. One way to find a part-time bookkeeper is to call the colleges in your area and ask if any students majoring in accounting are seeking work experience.

RECORDING YOUR INCOME

One of the most important functions of your record-keeping system is to provide an accurate record of the sources and amounts of income generated by your business. This is essential not only for tax-reporting purposes but for decision-making purposes as well. At the bare minimum, the income records for your network marketing business must include a cash receipts journal. If you extend credit to your customers, you will also need an accounts receivable journal.

Cash Receipts Journal

The cash receipts journal shown on page 156 illustrates how a network marketing business (in this case one that

CASH RECEIPTS JOURNAL

PLAYHOUSE TOYS
April 19XX

		1	2	3	4
Date	Customer Name	Educ.Toys	Books	Games	Audio Cassettes
4 / 3	Howard Domingo			9500	
4 / 4	Mary Ann Schwartz	7900			
4 / 5	Greg Adams		6000		
4 / 7	Linda Boggs	8500			4500

sells children's toys) can simply and easily keep track of its income flow. Recording the date, source, and amount of income earned, the cash receipts journal indicates which products are most in demand. Thus, in addition to providing you with the income figures required by the Internal Revenue Service, the journal provides valuable information about your target market. After a few months of recording your cash receipts in this way, you should know who your best customers are and which products or services are your best sellers.

The owner of the toy business sells: educational toys, books, games, and audio cassettes. Yet, the cash receipts journal shows that the income from the educational toys far exceeds the income from any of the other products.

Accounts Receivable Journal

Whenever possible, customers should be required to pay for their purchases at the time the sale is made. This gives you the immediate use of the funds and eliminates the need to collect later. However, if it's necessary to

ACCOUNTS RECEIVABLE JOURNAL

PLAYHOUSE TOYS

			Amount Due	30 Days Past Due	60 Days Past Due	90 Days Past Due
Date Due	Description/Name	Date Rec'd				
3/15	John Lewis		30000	✓	✓	
4/21	Peggy Smith	4/20	20000	--	--	--
4/30	Joseph Krueger	4/30	17500	--	--	--
5/17	Nancy Miller		22500			

allow your customers to buy on credit, then it's vital that you maintain an accounts receivable journal similar to the one shown above. This will provide a record of each sale and enable you to keep track of the money that is owed you. Then, when you receive payment, you can enter the income in your cash receipts journal, as shown on page 156.

BUSINESS EXPENSES

The record-keeping system for your network marketing business must provide you with a record of tax-deductible business expenses. To make this system work, you will have to determine precisely which expenses legitimately can be termed "business expenses." In the words of the Internal Revenue Service, "To be deductible, a business expense must be ordinary in your business and necessary for its operation." According to the IRS, "The word *ordinary* refers to the expense that is common and accepted practice in the industry. *Necessary* expenses are those that are appropriate and helpful in developing and maintaining your business." Thus, an expense that meets both parts of this test is deductible. Just a few of the expenses that meet these criteria include:

- Accounting services
- Advertising
- Attorney's fees
- Automobile expenses
- Business publications
- Charitable contributions
- Club dues
- Consultants' fees
- Credit reports
- Depreciation
- Entertainment
- Freight charges
- Insurance
- Interest
- Licenses
- Maintenance
- Meeting-room rentals
- Messenger service
- Newsletters
- Postage
- Publicity
- Rent
- Safe deposit box
- Salaries
- Seminars
- Stationery
- Supplies
- Taxes
- Travel
- Utilities

In calculating your business expenses, it's important to separate them from your personal expenses. For instance, travel expenses on a business trip are deductible, but the same expenses on a vacation are not. Taking a customer or potential network member to lunch is deductible; going to lunch with a friend purely for social reasons is not. Postage on Christmas cards sent to customers is deductible; postage on the cards sent to friends and relatives is not. In the event that an expense is partly for business and partly personal, only the business part is deductible. For example, if you go on a trip for both business and pleasure, you can deduct only the business portion of the trip, that is, if you take a client out to lunch and visit a museum with your family in the afternoon, only the lunch is deductible.

Cash Disbursement Journal

The best way to keep track of your expenses is to enter them in a cash disbursements journal like the one shown below. Make sure to record the following information:

* Date the expense was incurred
* Name of person or business receiving payment
* Check number
* Amount of check
* Category of business expense

When you set up your expense categories, arrange them in either alphabetical order or in the order in which they will appear on your tax forms. This will make it easier for you to locate the information later and transfer it to your tax forms when preparing your in-

CASH DISBURSEMENTS JOURNAL

PLAYHOUSE TOYS
April 19XX

Date	Description/Name	CK#	1 Accounting	2 Advertising	3 Automobile	4 Office Supplies
4/3	Jean Brown	645	250 00			
4/5	Daily Times	646		195 00		
4/7	Auto Dealer	647			95 00	
4/10	ABC Stationers	648				74 00

come tax return. At the end of each month, it's also a good idea to add up the expenses in each category to determine exactly where your money is going. This should help you to stay within your budget and to keep unnecessary expenses to a minimum.

Home Business Expenses

If your network marketing business is located in your home, you may be entitled to deduct a portion of the operating expenses and the depreciation on your home. To qualify for this deduction, the IRS stipulates that part of your home must be set aside *regularly* and *exclusively* for the business. In this regard, the space must be used as either (1) your principal place of business or (2) a place to meet and deal with customers or clients in the normal course of your business.

If your business occupies a free-standing structure next to your home—a studio, garage, or barn, for example—its expenses are deductible if you use the space regularly and exclusively for the business. In this case, the structure does not have to be your principal place of business or used to meet customers.

Figuring Your Home Deduction

To figure what percentage of your home-operating expenses and depreciation is deductible, use either of the following two methods:

1. Divide the area used for your business by the total area of your home.

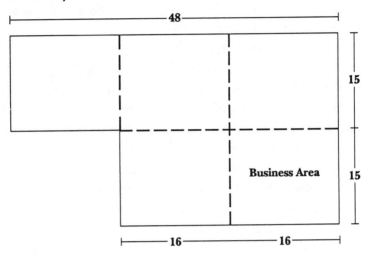

Business Area = 15 × 16 = 240 sq. ft.
Total Area = (15 × 48) + (15 × 32) = 1200 sq. ft.
Tax-deductible Area $= \dfrac{240}{1200} = \dfrac{1}{5} = 20$ percent

2. Divide the number of rooms used for your business by the number of rooms in your home.

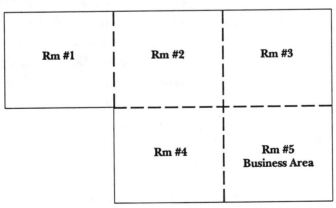

$$\dfrac{\text{Business Rooms}}{\text{Total Rooms}} = \dfrac{1}{5} = 20 \text{ percent}$$

You may find that the second method of figuring the tax-deductible area is easier. In order for the designations to be accurate, however, all of the rooms in your home must be approximately the same size.

Once you've determined the percentage of your home expenses that is deductible, multiply this figure by each expense in order to obtain the dollar amounts of your deductions. (For example, 20 percent of a $1,000 home utilities expense equals a $200 business-utilities expense). Those expenses that benefit only your business, such as painting or remodeling the specific area occupied by the business, are 100 percent deductible. Expenses that benefit only your home and are in no way related to the business, such as lawn care and landscaping, may *not* be deducted.

To make certain that you have accurately defined those expenses that benefit (1) both your home and your business, (2) only your business, and (3) only your home, it's advisable to consult with an accountant (particularly if you own, rather than rent, your home). If you decide to sell your home, the home expense deductions you've taken for the business will affect how and when capital gains on the sale are to be recognized. For more information on selling your home when a part of it is used as a business, check IRS publication number 523, "Tax Information on Selling Your Home."

Automobile Expenses

If you use an automobile or truck in your business, those expenses resulting from the business use of the vehicle are deductible. These expenses include gasoline, oil, maintenance and repairs, insurance, depreciation, interest on car payments, parking fees, taxes, license fees, and tolls.

Calculating Your Deductible Automobile Expenses

There are two ways to calculate your deductible automobile expenses: (1) using a standard mileage rate and (2) deducting a percentage of the total operating costs.

1. *Standard Mileage Rate.* To calculate your deductible automobile expenses using this method, keep a record of all miles you drive for business reasons during the year. Then multiply your total business mileage by the current rate allowed by the IRS. This will give you the dollar amount of your automobile expenses:

> Business Miles
> × Standard IRS Mileage Rate
> _____
> = Deductible Automobile Expense
>   (Parking fees and tolls may be added to this.)

The applicable rates are subject to change by the IRS. For more information, check IRS publication number 917, "Business Use of a Car."

2. *Percentage of Total Operating Costs.* To calculate your deductible automobile expenses this way, keep a record of the total number of miles driven in a year and the total number of miles you drive for business reasons during that year, *and* keep track of *all* your automobile expenses. Then (1) calculate the deductible percentage that the number of business miles is of the total mileage and (2) multiply the deductible percentage of automobile expenses by the total cost of operating your car.

Suppose in a particular year you drove 20,000 miles

of which 12,000 miles were for business purposes, and your total operating costs were $5,000. Then,

1. $\dfrac{12{,}000 \quad \text{Business Miles}}{20{,}000 \quad \text{Total Miles Driven}} = 60 \text{ percent}$

2. $\begin{array}{ll} \$5{,}000 & \text{Total Automobile Operating Costs} \\ \times\ 0.60 & \text{Deductible Percentage} \end{array}$

   $\begin{array}{ll} \$3{,}000 & \text{Deductible Automobile Expense} \end{array}$
   (Parking Fees and tolls may be added to this)

Since this method is based on your actual automobile operating costs rather than on a standard rate per mile, it's especially important to keep receipts documenting your automobile expenses.

To make sure that you are claiming the full automobile deduction the IRS allows, you should calculate your deductible using both of these methods (at least in the beginning). Then, after comparing the totals, choose the method that gives you the higher deduction.

Entertainment Expenses

Business entertainment expenses also are tax deductible. To qualify as a deductible item, the entertainment expense must be "ordinary and necessary" in carrying on your trade or operating your business. As with home business expenses and automobile expenses, you must separate your business expenses from the nonbusiness ones. Whenever entertainment is for both business and social purposes, only the business part is deductible. For example, if you entertain a group that includes three business prospects and one social guest, you may deduct the expenses for yourself and the three prospects, but you may *not* deduct the amount you spend on the social guest.

In determining whether or not an entertainment expense is deductible, ask yourself if the entertainment had a clear business purpose. Was it to get new business or to encourage the continuation of an existing business relationship? If your answer is yes, then you should be able to claim the expense as a business deduction. For example, taking a prospective customer to lunch or dinner is a deductible expense if you discuss business at some time during the meal.

To comply with the IRS rules on entertainment deductions, you should keep a record of all business entertainment expenses along with the receipts or other supporting evidence to back them up. Entering a luncheon date on your desk calendar isn't enough. To be properly documented, the lunch must be backed up by the receipt for the meal.

To claim an expense as a business entertainment deduction, you must be able to prove the following:

1. The amount of the expense
2. The date the entertainment took place
3. The location of the entertainment (such as a restaurant or theater)
4. The reason for the entertainment (to make a sale, to discuss your business with a prospective network member)
5. The name and title (or occupation) of each person you entertained.

The more specific you can be, the better, since this will add to the validity of your deductions.

YOUR TAXES

As much as you might want to ignore them, taxes are an inevitable part of business. If you keep good records, taxes shouldn't pose a problem. The nature of your network marketing business, its legal form, and its location will determine the taxes you pay.

Federal Taxes

The two best-known taxes that network marketers are required to pay are income tax and self-employment tax. If you employ other people in your business or you sell certain types of goods, you may also be subject to employment taxes and excise taxes.

Income Tax

Every business is required by law to file an annual income tax return. The form you use for this depends on whether your business is (1) a sole proprietorship, (2) a partnership, or (3) a corporation.

1. *Sole Proprietorship.*   If you are a sole proprietorship, you should report your business income and deductions on Schedule C (1040). Attach this schedule to your individual tax return Form 1040 and submit them together. If you own more than one business, you must file a separate Schedule C for each one.

2. *Partnership.*   If you are a partner in a network marketing business, your income and deductions from the partnership should be reported on Schedule K-1 (Form 1065) and filed along with your individual tax return. Each of your partners should do the same, accounting for his or her income and deductions in this way. In

addition to this, the total income and deductions for the partnership itself must be reported on Form 1065.

3. *Corporation.* A corporation reports its taxable income on Form 1120. S corporations use Form 1120S. Any income or dividends that you receive from the corporation should be entered on your individual tax return. However, if you are a shareholder in an S corporation, your income and deductions should be reported in the same way that they would be in a partnership. In this instance, though, you use Schedule K-1 (Form 1120S).

Self-Employment Tax

Self-employment tax is a Social Security tax for people who are self-employed. It's similar to the Social Security tax paid by wage earners, but you pay it yourself instead of having it withheld from your paycheck. As a network marketer, you must pay self-employment tax if you have net earnings from your business of $400 or more a year. To find out more about this tax, check IRS publication number 533, "Self-Employment Tax."

Estimated Tax

The IRS requires that you pay your income and self-employment taxes each year on a pay-as-you-go basis. Rather than paying them in one lump sum at the end of the tax period, you must estimate them in advance and pay them in installments by these dates:

- April 15
- June 15
- September 15
- January 15 (of the following year)

Using this method, you pay one-quarter of your total tax liability on each date until the liability is paid in full. If you discover (say, in August) that you are paying too much or too little tax, you can decrease or increase the size of the remaining payments. Remember, however, that you are required to prepay at least 90 percent of your tax liability each year. If you prepay less than this, you may be subject to a penalty.

Try to make your estimates as accurate as possible to spare yourself the expense of a penalty. When in doubt, pay *more* than the amount you've estimated to ensure meeting the 90 percent prepayment minimum. The form you use to estimate your tax is Form 1040-ES, which can be obtained from the IRS.

Employment Taxes

If you have employees in your network marketing business, you will probably need to pay employment taxes. These taxes include:

1. Federal income tax, which you withhold from your employees' wages
2. Social Security tax, part of which you withhold from your employees' wages and the rest of which you contribute as an employer
3. Federal unemployment tax, which you as an employer must pay

Report both income tax and the Social Security tax on Form 941, and pay both taxes when you submit the forms. Report and pay the federal unemployment tax separately, using Form 940. For more information about employment taxes and which ones, if any, you must pay, read IRS publication number 15, "Circular E."

Excise Taxes

Any tax that is selective in nature, singling out some products or services for taxation but not others, is known as an excise tax. Although it's not likely that you will have to pay any excise taxes, you should be aware of their existence. Excise taxes come in a variety of categories: some excise taxes are levied on the production or sale of certain goods, while others are imposed on specific kinds of services or businesses. For example, an insurance agent who handles policies issued by foreign insurers would have to pay excise taxes on those policies. A network marketer who sells fishing equipment may also be liable for excise taxes.

As you can see, the subject of excise taxes is clearly a mixed bag. To determine whether your product or service is subject to excise taxes, check your MLM company's handbook or study IRS publication number 510, "Excise Taxes." This will give you the information you need about excise taxes, along with an explanation of the procedures for reporting them.

State and Local Taxes

The types and amounts of state and local taxes you, as a network marketer, must pay will depend on where your business is located. For instance, businesses in New York and California are subject to higher rates of taxation than those in Pennsylvania and Texas. Some states have income and sales taxes, whereas others don't. All states have unemployment taxes.

Just as the states vary when it comes to taxation, so do counties, cities, and towns within the states. Some of the taxes imposed at this level include business taxes, licensing fees, and income taxes.

To make sure that your business is meeting its state and local tax obligations, contact the authorities for your locality to determine those taxes for which you are responsible.

IRS TAX PUBLICATIONS

The publications listed below can provide you with additional information about business taxation. These publications should be available at your local IRS office; if not, you can obtain them by writing to the Internal Revenue Service, Washington, DC 20224.

TITLE	Number
Your Rights as a Taxpayer	1
Employer's Tax Guide (Circular E)	15
Your Federal Income Tax	17
Tax Guide for Small Business	334
Fuel Tax Credits and Refunds	378
Travel, Entertainment, and Gift Expenses	463
Tax Withholding and Estimated Tax	505
Excise Taxes	510
Tax Information on Selling Your Home	523
Taxable and Nontaxable Income	525
Charitable Contributions	526
Residential Rental Property	527
Miscellaneous Deductions	529
Tax Information for Homeowners	530
Self-Employment Tax	533
Depreciation	534
Business Expenses	535
Accounting Periods and Methods	538
Tax Information on Partnerships	541
Tax Information on Corporations	542
Sale and Other Dispositions of Assets	544
Interest Expense	545

TITLE	Number
Nonbusiness Disasters, Casualties, and Thefts	547
Investment Income and Expenses	550
Basis of Assets	551
Recordkeeping for Individuals	552
Federal Tax Information on Community Property	555
Examinations of Returns, Appeal Rights, and Claims for Refund	556
Retirement Plans for the Self-Employed	560
Taxpayers Starting a Business	583
The Collection Process (Income Tax Accounts)	586A
Business Use of Your Home	587
Tax Information on S Corporations	589
Individual Retirement Arrangements (IRAs)	590
Guide to Free Tax Services	910
Tax Information for Direct Sellers	911
Business Use of a Car	917
Employment Taxes for Household Employers	926
Business Reporting	937
Filing Requirements for Employee Benefit Plans	1048

11

Keeping Your Business on Track

During the initial stages of starting a business, the primary concern is momentum—getting the business going and keeping it going. Each new customer served, each new network member recruited, each dollar earned represents a giant step, bringing you closer to that dream of success. But, as you accomplish your goals and set new ones, you'll begin to see that the road to success has a number of twists and turns. Rather than just charging straight ahead as fast as you can, you must sometimes slow down or change direction slightly as you make key decisions to keep your network marketing business on track.

To avoid making costly mistakes or experiencing major setbacks, among the questions you should ask yourself are:

- How many first-level distributors can I work with effectively at one time?

- Do I want to take on additional MLM company product lines?
- Should I change from one company to another?
- Do I want to branch out into other regions or keep the business local?
- Should I join forces with other network marketers to do joint promotions?
- Am I meeting the needs of my target market?
- Are there other target markets I should serve?
- What new opportunities should I pursue?
- What are my personal priorities?
- What new challenges appeal to me?

KEY DECISION AREAS

The areas in which you must be prepared to make key decisions about your network marketing business include: structure and size, product offerings, promotion methods, target market, and direction.

Structure and Size

In looking at the structure and size of your business, you must decide how you want it to grow and how large a geographic area you want to cover.

Shaping Your Network

The first thing to consider as you recruit network members is the number of first-level distributors you can work with effectively at any one time. Although it's tempting to sign up as many people as you can, there's a limit to the number you can interact with at one time and still manage to provide the guidance and support each member of your group needs. If you make the mistake of overloading your first level, you'll find yourself being unable to adequately train the people you recruit.

In management parlance, the number of people you can effectively supervise is called your *span of control.* Depending on a person's management skills and experience, as well as the capabilities of the people being supervised, one's span of control can be narrow or wide, encompassing a handful of people or many. There is no set number that's right for everyone. One person may feel that the ideal number of people to directly supervise is five; another person may say ten is best. Thus, as your network grows, you must evaluate—and reevaluate—the number of people with whom you feel comfortable working on a one-on-one basis. Naturally, this figure can vary with the amount of time you have available to spend with representatives and the recruitment and training skills of the people themselves.

As a general rule, you will be better off to expand your network vertically (downward) rather than horizontally (sideways). This means sponsoring fewer new members yourself and spending more time helping those you do bring in to build their own networks, thereby adding additional levels to your organization. In other words, instead of building a "flat" network that looks like this:

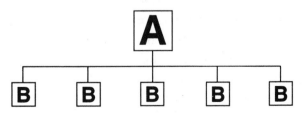

You would build a "deep" network that looks like this:

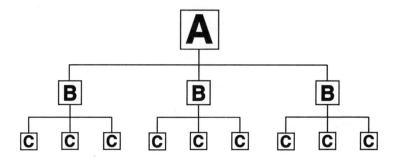

Then, once you've helped a distributor to begin building his or her own network and feel confident that the person can work independently, you can bring in another first-level distributor and get him or her started, repeating the process again and again.

Expanding Your Sales Market

In addition to making decisions about the growth rate and structure of your network marketing organization, you must also decide whether you want to keep it a local business or branch out into other regions. Part of this decision may be made for you as network members move to other cities and states and want to continue as representatives, in which case you would find yourself expanding your business whether you planned to or not. A different issue, however, is the geographic expansion that you actively direct yourself, entering underrepresented regions where the MLM company products you sell weren't previously available.

Expanding your sales market in this way can be very profitable, especially if you decide to capitalize on the opportunities that arise when an MLM company you represent begins operating in a new state or even in a new country. In both of these instances, established representatives with a good understanding of network marketing methods would be at an advantage when it comes to developing the new regions.

Expanding into a new region isn't without its drawbacks, and the decision to do so is a critical one. Offsetting the additional profits to be made are the increased expenditures for travel, communications (telephone, fax, promotional materials, and so on), and support staff. And there is the risk that, by having a larger sales market to cover, you may end up neglecting customers or network members, causing your overall business to suffer.

Product Offerings

In terms of the products or services you offer, the decisions you must make include whether to: (1) offer an MLM company's entire line or selected portions of it; (2) carry the lines of more than one MLM company; or (3) change companies altogether, switching to an MLM company you believe shows greater promise.

Which Products to Carry?

When it comes to choosing which products to carry, be they from one or more companies, the important thing is to pick those products that you feel are best suited to the needs of your target market. There's no sense in offering products or services for which there is little or no demand; nor do you want to invest in unnecessary inventory. Thus, in evaluating product offerings, you must carefully determine which are appropriate for you to represent and which are not.

Single Line or Multiple Lines?

As for representing more than one MLM company, as long as this is done in accordance with the policies and procedures of the companies involved, you may find this expansion a viable option. From a logistics standpoint, however, you must consider the decision carefully. Since the sales commissions and bonuses that MLM companies pay out are linked to volume, by spreading your personal and group sales over more than one company's product line, you may reduce the commission rates that you and your network members receive. Also, while you would be dividing your selling and promotion efforts among different product lines, you would create extra work for yourself and could confuse customers with too many product lines. And, if some of the members in your network elect not to carry the multiple-product lines, this staff division could affect your working relationships and disrupt your group unity.

On the positive side, by having more than one company's product line to offer customers, you may be better able to serve them. Multiple-product lines also offer the advantage of giving you something to fall back on if the sales of one company's product offering should fall off or be subject to cyclical fluctuations throughout the year.

As you can see, in making the decision of how many MLM companies' product lines to carry, you must weigh the pros and cons of both alternatives—single line versus multiple lines. It's also a good idea to get your network members' views on the matter, rather than deciding to take on an additional product line without consulting them.

For help in determining whether an MLM company's products or services should be added to your current product offering or not, use the New Product Evaluation Table shown below:

NEW PRODUCT EVALUATION TABLE				
Product Characteristics	**Excellent**	**Good**	**Fair**	**Poor**
1. Compatibility with current products/ services				
2. Compatibility with the business's image				
3. Level of consumer demand				
4. Profit potential				
5. Competitive strength				
6. Obtainability				
7. Promotability				
8. Uniqueness				
9. Product Safety				
10. Compliance with legal requirements				
11. MLM company's support				
12. MLM company's reputation				

When to Change Companies?

Deciding whether or not to drop your affiliation with an MLM company is perhaps the hardest of all the business decisions you might make. Since the decision affects not only you, but all the members in your network, you must consider the decision to leave a company as carefully as you considered joining it.

Just because an MLM company might be going through a difficult phase (expansion, developing new products, or a reorganization, for example), this is not necessarily a reason to change companies. If you still believe in the company's products or services and feel that the company can solve its problems, try to be patient and look beyond the current difficulties. On the other hand, if you've lost confidence in the product offering or don't think that you can work well with the company, then a change might be in order.

Whatever you decide, make sure that you include your network members in the decision-making process and inform them of the reasons for your decision. And, if you *do* decide to switch to another company, try to get as many network members as you can to move with you to keep your group as intact as possible.

Promotion Methods

The major decisions to make concerning your promotion methods are: which methods to use, when and where to use promotions, what message you want to communicate, and how much money to spend. As noted in Chapter 4, there are a number of methods you can use—both paid-for (advertising) and free (publicity)—

to promote your business. Be aware, however, that, as your network marketing business changes over time, its promotional needs, as well as the most effective promotion methods, can change, too. A method that worked before may no longer be appropriate, or a way of communicating that wasn't previously available (such as by computer or fax machine) may now present a way to increase the efficiency of communication.

To keep your business on track, your task is to determine the most cost-effective means of getting the attention of the people in your target market. You also have to determine the information you want to convey—personalized service, quality products, convenience, lower prices, and so on—and how you want to space your promotions throughout the year. By being open to new promotion ideas and methods, you can make sure that your products or services stay in the public eye.

Target Market

Two of the most important decisions any businessperson can make are (1) what target markets to serve and (2) what customer needs to satisfy. In order for your network marketing business to live up to its potential, you must become adept at recognizing what your customers want and spotting new customers who can benefit from your product offering.

All too often, network marketers become complacent, assuming that because their customers wanted certain products before, they must still want them now. Or, once having identified a target market for their products, some network marketers don't seek out other markets that might be profitable for them. As a result, they find their businesses stagnating, instead of grow-ing, and complain that "nobody's buying anymore."

One way to avoid stagnation is to be closely attuned to your customers' lives—find out out what's important to them, how they spend their time, and what you can do to make their lives better. If saving time is important to your customers, you could make it easier for them to buy from you by putting on sales presentations at their homes or places of business. Or, if the members of your target market are going through major changes in their lives—reentering the workforce, moving from one age group to the next, going from being parents with children at home to becoming "empty nesters," and so on—you should anticipate what their new needs will be and offer products they can really use at their new stage of life.

You can also find opportunities by being on the lookout for new target markets to interest in your products or services. For example, corporate America has turned out to be a good target market for the cosmetics and image-consulting fields, hiring network marketers to put on workshops for their employees. And now that people are marrying later, the market for fine china and crystal—which once was almost exclusively couples—includes a large portion of singles, many of them men.

Direction

In choosing the direction you want your network mar-keting business to take, you must also choose a direction for yourself. Do you want to run your business as a sideline that provides you with extra income or do you want to run it as a full-time enterprise? Do you want to get your children involved in the business and have them take over some of the day-to-day responsibilities? Do you want to widen or narrow the focus of your business to make it more responsive to customers' needs or to capitalize on specific opportunities that would be more personally fulfilling to you?

To assist you in discovering what you want to do next, use the New Challenge Rating Scale on page 184 to pinpoint the direction(s) in which to go.

LONG-RANGE PLANNING

In addition to setting goals and creating action plans for achieving them (both of which are short-range planning activities), to keep your network marketing business on track, you need to engage in long-range planning. Whereas short-range plans, or *tactics*, cover a period of a year or less, long-range plans, or *strategies*, typically cover a period from two to five years or longer. As such, they're the critical next step in guiding your business where you want it to go.

Network marketers (and other entrepreneurs) who succeed tend to be hard workers, good problem solvers, alert spotters of new opportunities, and savvy risk takers. In many instances, though, they have had little experience with planning. Their businesses were converted into realities through action, not planning. As the businesses grow, however, and the number and magnitude of decisions to be made increases, the need for a long-range plan takes on new importance.

NEW CHALLENGE RATING SCALE			
	Priority		
New Challenges	**Low**	**Medium**	**High**
1. Increasing sales			
2. Building the network			
3. Promoting business			
4. Expanding into other regions			
5. Entering a new field			
6. Gaining recognition			
7. Becoming an industry leader			
8. Improving management skills			
9. Improving motivation skills			
10. Making better use of time			
11. Being creative			
12. Getting family involved			
13. Helping others			
14. Planning for retirement			
15.			
16.			

Your Business Plan

The following steps should help you to prepare your business plan or modify an existing one.

Step 1: Define the nature of your network marketing business and its ultimate objectives.   For instance, you might state that yours is a gourmet-foods business and its ultimate objectives are to (1) be known for its line of quality frozen foods, (2) have a reputation for dependable service, (3) increase food sales by 20 percent per year, and (4) expand into related tableware products (placemats, napkins, table decorations).

Step 2: Communicate your objectives to those network members and others (your sponsor, employees, accountant, and so on) whose help you need to realize your objectives.   In this way, rather than working in the dark or at cross purposes, everyone can join forces for maximum results. This step also enables you to get feedback, which might have a bearing on your overall strategy, and helps to create a sense of belonging among the members of your network.

Step 3: Forecast or predict the future, based on the data available (your own observations, surveys, government reports, the media, and so on).   Your purpose in forecasting is to discover new trends that might affect the demand for your product or service. In the case of your frozen gourmet-foods business, you might discover that with more women working, the demand for frozen gourmet foods is going up because working women have more money to spend and less time to cook. You may also discover that, by providing the tableware products as well, you can better serve your target market, providing one-stop shopping for their entertaining needs.

Step 4: Inventory your resources for achieving your objectives. This means taking stock of your assets—those that show up on a balance sheet and those that don't. Do you have the equipment and space you will need to handle the added sales volume and the additional product line? Do you have the knowledge and commitment to carry out all the tasks associated with your objectives? If not, will you be able to obtain the resources you need?

Step 5: Set intermediate goals and a timetable for achieving your objectives.   This means outlining the sequence of events that must take place to reach your destination. To continue the gourmet-foods example, if you decide to expand your frozen-food business into the tablewares area, you must do the following: (1) find a reputable MLM company to supply the products you want, (2) obtain promotional materials for the new line, (3) interest network members in carrying it, and (4) set up a separate recordkeeping system to monitor the sales and commissions it generates.

By taking the time to formulate your objectives in this way and to map out a strategy for achieving them, you will be better prepared to capitalize on any opportunities that arise and to keep your network marketing business positioned for success.

SUCCESS ON YOUR OWN TERMS

In setting the objectives for your business, it's absolutely essential to set your own personal objectives as well. What do you as an individual want? Will making your network marketing business a success make you a personal success, too?

Probably as much has been written about the high price of success as the joys of attaining it. The price can be strained personal relationships, stress, impaired

PERSONAL SUCCESS INDICATORS

Success Indicators	Very Important	Moderately Important	Relatively Unimportant
1. Financial security	_____	_____	_____
2. Good health	_____	_____	_____
3. Challenging work	_____	_____	_____
4. Opportunity to be creative	_____	_____	_____
5. Time to myself	_____	_____	_____
6. Time with my family	_____	_____	_____
7. Good friends	_____	_____	_____
8. Control over my environment	_____	_____	_____
9. Recognition from my family	_____	_____	_____
10. Recognition from my peers	_____	_____	_____
11. Recognition from the public	_____	_____	_____
12. An affluent lifestyle	_____	_____	_____
13. An active social life	_____	_____	_____
14. Opportunity to learn	_____	_____	_____
15. Being able to travel	_____	_____	_____
16. Involvement in civic activities	_____	_____	_____
17. Looking my best	_____	_____	_____
18. A well-run home	_____	_____	_____
19. Able to make a difference	_____	_____	_____
20. Spiritual well-being	_____	_____	_____

health, the feeling that you're missing out on something or aren't appreciated, lack of time for yourself, or worse. But, if you strive for a realistic balance between caring for your business and caring for yourself and family and friends, you won't fall into these traps.

The more closely your personal objectives match those of your business, the lower the price of success. If you become involved in a business that enables you to satisfy your needs, rather than demanding that you sacrifice them, you will be both happy *and* successful.

Keeping in mind what you will have to do to achieve the objectives you've set for your business, stop and think about the things you want for yourself and how important they are to you. Then use the Personal Success Indicators chart on page 187 to rate each one.

If, in satisfying your business objectives, you can also satisfy your most important personal needs, then you've found the way to have success on your own terms.

12

Multilevel Marketing Companies

To learn more about multilevel marketing, consult the following listings of trade associations and companies in the multilevel/direct sales field. In most cases, the name of a reference person is provided.

If you would like to know about a company that isn't listed or want to get an individual assessment of a company you are considering, it's a good idea to contact the trade associations shown here.

ASSOCIATIONS

Direct Selling Association
1776 K Street NW, Washington, DC 20006
Telephone: (202) 293-5760

Multi-Level Marketing International Association
119 Stanford Court, Irvine, CA 92715
Doris Wood
Telephone: (714) 854-5488

COMPANIES

Act II Jewelry, Inc.–Lady Remington
818 Thorndale Avenue, Bensenville, IL 60106
John E. Kiple
Telephone: (708) 860-3323
Jewelry (fashion and fine)

Alfa Metalcraft Corporation of America
GOS International Distributors, Inc.
6593 Powers Avenue Suite 17, Jacksonville, FL 32217
Terence Fredricks or Gonzalo Oliva
Telephone: (904) 731-8200
Cookware

Aloette Cosmetics, Inc.
345 Lancaster Avenue, Malvern, PA 19355
John E. Defibaugh
Telephone: (215) 644-8200
Cosmetics, skin care products

American-i-can Fire and Safety Corporation
314 West Lincoln Highway, Penndel, PA 19047
Greg H. Landau
Telephone: (215) 750-7373
Fire extinguishers

American Horizons
11251 Phillips Parkway Drive East, Jacksonville, FL 32224
Patricia McGaffey
Telephone: (904) 260-4911
Cosmetics, skin care products

America's Buyers, Inc.
339 East 16th Street, Holland, MI 49423
Telephone: (616) 392-7141
Buyer's club

American 3-D Corporation
15 Cactus Garden Drive, Henderson, NV 89014
James Song
Telephone: (702) 454-7000
3-D Cameras

Amway Corporation
7575 East Fulton Road, Ada, MI 49355
Casey Wondergem
Telephone: (616) 676-6000
Household, personal, homecare, nutrition products; catalog

Artistic Impressions, Inc.
236 East Adele Court, Villa Park, IL 60181
Bart Breighner
Telephone: (708) 833-8200
Art

Avacare, Inc., Division of Nutri-Metics International
19501 East Walnut Drive, City of Industry, CA 91749
Telephone: (714) 598-1831
Cosmetics—skin, hair, health care products

Avadyne, Inc.
2801 Salinas Highway, Bldg. F, Monterey, CA 93940
James A. Coover
Telephone: (408) 373-2300
Meal replacement formula and nutrition-related products

Avon Products, Inc.
9 West 57th Street, New York, NY 10019
E.V. Goings
Telephone: (212) 546-6015
Cosmetics, jewelry

BeautiControl Cosmetics
PO Box 815189, Dallas, TX 75381
Telephone: (214) 458-0601
Cosmetics, image consulting

Bose Corporation
The Mountain Road, Framingham, MA 01701
Sherwin Greenblatt
Telephone: (508) 879-7330
Acoustic wave music

Brite Music Enterprises, Inc.
Box 9191, Salt Lake City, UT 84109
W. Edward Brady
Telephone: (801) 487-8371
Children's song books, cassettes, records

The Bron-Shoe Company
1313 Alum Creek Drive, Columbus, OH 43209
Robert J. Kaynes, Jr.
Telephone: (614) 252-0967
Baby-shoe bronzing

Cameo Coutures, Inc.
9004 Ambassador Row, Dallas, TX 75247
J. Stanley Fredrick
Telephone: (214) 631-4860
Clothing—lingerie, loungewear

Chambre' Cosmetics Corporation
10138 Huebner Road, PO Box 690370, San Antonio, TX 78240
Gayle C. McCracken
Telephone: (512) 694-0846
Cosmetics, food supplements

Club Watermasters, Inc. (Regal Ware, Inc.)
5670 West Cypress Street, Suite I, Tampa, FL 33607
George M. Carriker
Telephone: (813) 286-8939
Drinking-water systems

Collectors Corner, Inc. and Affiliates
5327 W. Minnesota Street, Indianapolis, IN 46241
Charles E. Swanson
Telephone: (317) 247-9716
Oil paintings, limited-edition prints

P. F. Collier, Inc., Educational Services Division
135 Community Drive, Great Neck, NY 11021
John J. Toman
Telephone: (516) 829-6100
Encyclopedias

Compuclub Marketing Group, Inc.
4901 Morena Blvd. Suite 402, San Diego, CA 92117
Telephone: (619) 483-6100
Computers (home), hardware and software

Contempo Fashions (The Gerson Company)
6100 Broadmoor, Shawnee Mission, KS 66202
Steven Shinderman
Telephone: (913) 262-7407
Jewelry, accessories

Country Home Collection
1719 Hallock-Young Road, Warren, OH 44481
Gerald E. Henn
Telephone: (216) 824-2052
Decorative home products

The Creative Circle
15711 South Broadway, Gardena, CA 90248
William T. Hultquist
Telephone: (213) 769-2480
Needlecraft products

Creative Memories
2815 Clearwater Road, PO Box 767, St. Cloud, MN 56302
Cheryl S. Lightle
Telephone: (612) 251-3822
Photo albums

CUTCO-Alcas Cutlery Corporation
1116 East State Street, PO Box 810, Olean, NY 14760
Donald R. Freda
Telephone: (716) 372-3111
Cutlery, cookware, tableware

D.E.L.T.A. International
16910 West 10 Mile Road, Suite 400, Southfield, MI 48076
Emily L. Sutton-Mlodzik
Telephone: (313) 559-1224
Nutritional products

Dexi US Inc.
6329 Peachtree Industrial Boulevard, Doraville, GA 30360
Deborah A. Templeton
Telephone: (404) 446-8677
Cosmetics

Diamite Corporation
1625 McCandless Drive, Milpitas, CA 95035
Rudy Revak
Telephone: (408) 945-1000
Nutritional and personal-care products

Discovery Toys, Inc.
2530 Arnold Drive, Suite 400, Martinez, CA 94553
Lane Nemeth
Telephone: (415) 370-7575
Toys (educational)—books, games

Doncaster
Oak Springs Road, Box 1159, Rutherfordton, NC 28139
Michael S. Tanner
Telephone: (704) 287-4205
Clothing—ladies' dresses, coats, outer/sportswear

Dudley Products Company
7856 McCloud Road, Greensboro, NC 27409
Joe Louis Dudley, Sr.
Telephone: (919) 668-3000
Cosmetics

Eagle Shield, Inc.
2006 North Highway 360, Grand Prairie, TX 75050
Antonio S. Duque or Virgil O. Barnard III
Telephone: (214) 641-9655
Radiant barrier

Earth Pride
490 East Main St., Lake Zurich, IL 60047
Tim Dern
Telephone: (708) 540-6770
Environmentally friendly, home/personal-care products

efe' Cosmetics, Ltd.
4940 El Camino Real, P.O. Box 329, Los Altos, CA 94022
Zane E. Seely
Telephone: (415) 961-5442
Natural nail care

Ekco Home Products Company
2382 Townsgate Road, Westlake Village, CA 91361
Ronald H. Franklin
Telephone: (805) 494-1711
Cookware and cutlery

Elan Vital, Ltd.
2700 East Sunset Road, Suite D-38, Pahrump, NV 89041
Karen Shulman
Telephone: (702) 798-0333
Vitamins, nutritional supplements

Electrolux Corporation
2300 Windy Ridge Parkway, Suite 900 South, Marietta, GA 30067
Steven D. Cooper
Telephone: (404) 933-1000
Vacuum cleaners, floor polishers

Emma Page Jewelry, Inc.
7 Deer Run, P.O. Box 179, Blairston, NJ 07825
Earl Sachs
Telephone: (201) 362-5999
Jewelry

Encyclopedia Britannica, Inc.
Britannica Centre, 310 South Michigan Avenue, Chicago, IL
  60604
Peter B. Norton
Telephone: (312) 347-7000
Educational publications

Energy Savers, Inc.
4320 Buffalo Road, Mt. Airy, MD 21771
Chester W. Sapalio
Telephone: (301) 775-2062
Energy barrier

Family Record Plan, Inc.
5155 North Clareton Drive, PO Box 3043, Agoura Hills, CA 91301
Alan F. Kane
Telephone: (818) 707-3380
Photography (professional and amateur)

Fiberline National Voice Mail
7220 Trade Street, San Diego, CA 92121
Paul Cohen
Telephone: (619) 689-0066
Communications equipment (advanced, state-of-the-art)

Financial Independence Club
3200 South Bristol Street #750, Costa Mesa, CA 92626
Sam Phan
Telephone: (714) 754-5755
Mortgages (bi-weekly)

Finelle Cosmetics
137 Marston Street, PO Box 5200, Lawrence, MA 01842
Maurice J. Feigenbaum
Telephone: (508) 682-6112
Cosmetics, skin care products

Fortunate Corporation
P.O. Box 5604, Charlottesville, VA 22905
Telephone: (804) 977-5720
Pet, personal-care, home-cleaning products, vitamins

ForYou, Inc.
4235 Main Street, PO Box 1216, Loris, SC 29569
Winferd D. Holt
Telephone: (803) 756-9000
Skin-care products

The Fuller Brush Company
5635 Hanes Mill Road, Winston-Salem, NC 27105
Derek J. Stryker
Telephone: (919) 744-4300
Household/personal-care items

Golden Pride, Inc.–W.T. Rawleigh
1501 Northpoint Parkway, Suite 100, West Palm Beach, FL 33407
Betsy Stockdill
Telephone: (407) 640-5700
Health and beauty aids

Grolier Incorporated
Sherman Turnpike, Danbury, CT 06816
Keith George
Telephone: (203) 797-3500
Educational publications

The Hanover Shoe, Inc.
118 Carlisle Street, Hanover, PA 17331
Joseph M. Halko
Telephone: (717) 632-7575
Shoes (men's and women's)

Health-Mor, Inc.
151 East 22nd Street, Lombard, IL 60148
Shannon P. Burke
Telephone: (708) 953-9770
Vacuum cleaners (Filter Queen)

Heart and Home, Inc.
76 Commercial Way, East Providence, RI 02914
Andrew Anderson
Telephone: (401) 438-6668
Decorative accessories

Herbalife International
9800 La Cienega Boulevard, PO Box 80210, Los Angeles, CA
  90009
George E. Betts
Telephone: (213) 410-9600
Weight control and food products

Highlights for Children, Inc.
2300 West Fifth Avenue, PO Box 269, Columbus, OH 43215
Garry C. Myers
Telephone: (614) 486-0631
Educational publications—magazines

Hold Everything
4701 Alta Mesa, Forth Worth, TX 76133
David C. Rawls, Jr.
Telephone: (817) 294-1292
Clothing (women's)

Home Interiors & Gifts, Inc.
4550 Spring Valley Road, Dallas, TX 75244
Donald J. Carter
Telephone: (214) 386-1000
Decorative accessories

House of Lloyd, Inc.
11901 Grandview Road, Grandview, MO 64030
Harry J. Lloyd
Telephone: (816) 966-2222
Toys, gifts, Christmas decorations

Jafra Cosmetics, Inc.
PO Box 5026, Westlake Village, CA 91359
Robin H. Kirkland
Telephone: (805) 496-1911
Cosmetics, skin care products

Just America (Tanner Companies Inc.)
Oak Springs Road, Rutherfordton, NC 28139
Gordon Stagg
Telephone: (704) 287-4205
Skin care products (Swiss herbal)

The Kirby Company
1920 West 114th Street, Cleveland, OH 44102
Gene L. Windfeldt
Telephone: (216) 228-2400
Vacuum cleaners

Kitchen Fair
1090 Redmond Road, PO Box 100, Jacksonville, AR 72076
Gary R. Stephen
Telephone: (501) 982-7446
Cookware, kitchen, and decorative accessories

Lady Love Cosmetics
1515 Champion Drive, Carrollton, TX 75006
Jerry L. Lovelace
Telephone: (214) 484-3950
Cosmetics, skin care products

Learnex Ltd., Inc.
89 Saw Mill River Road, Elmsford, NY 10523
Telephone: (914) 592-1770
Children's books, cassettes, educational toys

Light Force
1115 Thompson Avenue, Suite 5, Santa Cruz, CA 95062
Pope McElvy
Telephone: (408) 462-5000
Nutritional supplements

Lonaberger Marketing
2503 Maple Avenue, Zanesville, OH 43701
Tamala L. Kaido
Telephone: (614) 455-3175
Baskets

Lucky Heart Cosmetics, Inc.
138 Huling Avenue, Memphis, TN 38103
Paul D. Shapiro
Telephone: (901) 526-7658
Cosmetics, jewelry

Magneto Hydro Dynamics, Inc.
30 Corporate Park #104, Irvine, CA 92714
Randy Ambrose
Telephone: (714) 250-5981
Magnetic fuel and water-conditioning units

Mary Kay Cosmetics, Inc.
8787 Stemmons Freeway, Dallas, TX 75247
Monty C. Barber
Telephone: (214) 630-8787
Cosmetics, skin care products

Matol Botanical Int'l Ltd
1111 46th Ave. #100, Lachine Quebec, Canada H8T 3C5
J. F. Robert Boduc
Telephone: (514) 745-6300
Dietary supplements

Melaleuca
560 Broadway Plaza, Idaho Falls, ID 83402
Frank Vandersloot
Telephone: (208) 522-0700
Skin care, home care, and nutrition products

Miracle Maid
(Rena-Ware Distributors), PO Box C-50, Redmond, WA 98052
Philip Lindquist
Telephone: (206) 881-6171
Cookware

National Safety Associates, Inc.
4260 East Raines Road, Memphis, TN 38118
Jay A. Martin
Telephone: (901) 366-9288
Water-treatment systems

Nature's Sunshine Products, Inc.
1655 North Main, PO Box 1000, Spanish Fork, UT 84660
Alan D. Kennedy
Telephone: (801) 798-9861
Herbs, vitamins, personal care products

Neo-Life Corporations of America
3500 Gateway Boulevard, PO Box 5012, Fremont, CA 94537
Jerry Brassfield
Telephone: (415) 651-0405
Household products, vitamins, minerals, food, water

Network 2000
14401 East 42nd Street, Independence, MO 64055
Jim Adams
Telephone: (816) 373-4600
Telephone long-distance services (U.S. Sprint)

Noevir, Inc.
1095 SE Main Street, Irvine, CA 92714
Wesley H. Miyahara
Telephone: (714) 660-1111
Cosmetics

Nu-Skin International, Inc.
145 East Center, Provo, UT 84601
Steven Lund
Telephone: (801) 377-6056
Cosmetics, health products

Nutri-Metics International, Inc.
19501 East Walnut Drive, City of Industry, CA 91749
Mulford J. Nobbs
Telephone: (714) 598-1831
Cosmetics, food supplements

Omnitrition International
PO Box 560208, Dallas, TX 75356
Charles E. Ragus
Telephone: (214) 630-8282
Nutritional products

Oriflame Corporation
76 Treble Cove Road, North Billerica, MA 01862
Peter A. Nawrocki
Telephone: (508) 663-2700
Cosmetics (European skin care)

Our Secret Creation
155 North San Vicente Blvd., Beverly Hills, CA 90211
Brian Riechenberg
Telephone: (213) 852-4896
Jewelry (unique and unusual)

The Pampered Chef, Inc.
PO Box 172, River Forest, IL 60305
Doris K. Christopher
Telephone: (708) 366-4059
Kitchenware

Parent & Child Resource Center, Inc. (Highlights for Children, Inc.)
2300 West Fifth Avenue, PO Box 269, Columbus, OH 43215
Patrick Clowes
Telephone: (614) 486-0631
Educational publications—magazines

Partylite Gifts
Building 16, Cordage Park, Plymouth, MA 02360
Elizabeth R. Montgomery
Telephone: (508) 746-6104
Decorative accessories

Personal Resource System, Inc.
1307 Stratford Court, PO Box 2529, Del Mar, CA 92014
Telephone: (619) 755-5664
Personal-organization, time-management system

Personal Wealth Systems
PO Box 17743, Jacksonville, FL 32245
Gary Haiser
Telephone: (904) 731-5785
Personal and financial development products/services

Petra Fashions, Inc.
33 Cherry Hill Drive, Danvers, MA 01923
Jonathan B. Hodges
Telephone: (508) 777-5853
Clothing—lingerie, sleepware

Pola U.S.A., Inc.
251 East Victoria Avenue, Carson, CA 90746
Shizuko Uragami
Telephone: (213) 770-6000
Cosmetics

Primerica Financial Services (Formerly A. L. Williams)
3100 Breckenridge Blvd., Duluth, GA 30199
Telephone: (404) 381-1674
Insurance and financial investments

Princess House, Inc.
455 Somerset Avenue, North Dighton, MA 02764
Richard C. Brown
Telephone: (508) 823-0713
Decorative accessories

Pro-Ag Inc.
2072 East Center Circle, Minneapolis, MN 55441
Bill Schmidt
Telephone: (612) 553-1130
Agricultural products (Impro/NU-AG)

PRO-MA Systems (U.S.A.), Inc.
976 Florida Central Parkway, Suite 136, Longwood, FL 32752
Gene Rumley
Telephone: (407) 331-1133
Cosmetics, skin care products

Regal Ware, Inc.
1675 Reigle Drive, Kewaskum, WI 53040
Gilbert D. Flocker
Telephone: (414) 626-2121
Cookware

Rena-Ware Distributors, Inc.
PO Box 97050, Redmond, WA 98073
Philip Lindquist
Telephone: (206) 881-6171
Cookware

Rich Plan Corporation
4981 Commercial Drive, Yorkville, NY 13495
Thomas R. Steinback
Telephone: (800) 243-1358
Frozen food, appliances

Rickshaw Imports (Wicker World Enterprises)
800 North Edgewood Avenue, Wood Dale, IL 60191
Madolyn J. Schwartz
Telephone: (708) 860-5452
Wicker accessories (decorative)

Saladmaster, Inc.
131 Howell Street, Dallas, TX 75207
J. William Francisco
Telephone: (214) 742-2222
Cookware, tableware

SASCO Products, Inc.
1515 Champion Drive, Carrollton, TX 75006
John T. Fleming
Telephone: (214) 484-3950
Cosmetics

Shaklee Corporation
Shaklee Terraces, 444 Market Street, San Francisco, CA 94111
Rakesh K. Kaul
Telephone: (415) 954-3000
Food supplements, personal care products

Society Corporation
1609 Kilgore Avenue, Muncie, IN 47305
Foster D. Adams
Telephone: (317) 289-3318
Cookware, china, crystal

The Southwestern Company
2451 Atrium Way, PO Box 305140, Nashville, TN 37230
Jerry Heffel
Telephone: (615) 391-2500
Educational publications

Spirit Plus (The Southwestern Co.)
PO Box 305140, Nashville, TN 37230
Eddy Messick
Telephone: (615) 391-2500
T-shirts (personally designed)

Stanhome Inc.
333 Western Avenue, Westfield, MA 01085
Bill Tower
Telephone: (413) 562-3631
Household cleaning and personal care products

Step's Adventures with the 3R's
8521 44 Avenue West, PO Box 887, Mukilteo, WA 98275
Telephone: (206) 355-9830
Educational programs—reading, math, perceptual tasks

Sunrider International
3111 Lomita Blvd., Torrance, CA 90505
Dr. Tei Fu Chen
Telephone: (213) 534-4786
Health-related products

Tandy Home Education Systems
1301 West 22nd Street, Suite 400, Oak Brook, IL 60521
Telephone: (312) 325-6150
Home computer systems

Tiara Exclusives
717 E Street, Dunkirk, IN 47336
Robert J. Staab
Telephone: (317) 768-7821
Decorative accessories, glassware

Time-Life Books, Inc.
777 Duke Street, Alexandria, VA 22314
Basil L. Ong
Telephone: (703) 838-7000
Educational publications

Tomorrow's Treasures, Inc.
111 North Glassboro Road, Woodbury Heights, NJ 08097
George W. Braun
Telephone: (609) 468-5656
Photo albums, photography

Tri-Chem, Inc.
One Cape May Street, Harrison, NJ 07029
Andrew D. McKnight
Telephone: (201) 482-5500
Craft products—liquid embroidery paint

Tupperware Home Parties
PO Box 2353, Orlando, FL 32802
Augustine J. English
Telephone: (407) 847-3111
Food-storage containers, cookware, children's toys (plastic)

U.S. Safety & Engineering Corporation
2365 El Camino Avenue, Sacramento, CA 95821
H. Wayne Boyd
Telephone: (916) 482-8888
Security systems—fire and burglar alarms

United Consumers Club, Inc.
8450 South Broadway, Merrillville, IN 46410
Fred A. Wittlinger
Telephone: (219) 736-1100
Buyers' service

United Laboratories of America, Inc.
1526 Fort Worth Avenue, PO Box 4499, Station A, Dallas, TX
    75208
Bill Sparks
Telephone: (214) 741-4461
Photo albums, Bibles, photo enlargements

Vita Craft Corporation
11100 West 58th Street, PO Box 3129, Shawnee, KS 66203
L. Dale Ashley
Telephone: (913) 631-6265
Cookware, china, crystal, tableware, cutlery

Viva America Marketing, Inc.
5426 East Slauson Avenue, Commerce, CA 90040
Jay Roberts
Telephone: (213) 888-2200
Personal care products, nutritional supplements

Vorwerk USA, Inc.
222 Westmont Drive South, Altamonte Springs, FL 32714
Jochen W. Sarrazin
Telephone: (407) 682-2255
Housewares—carpet and floor care equipment

Water Resources International, Inc.
2800 East Chambers Street, Phoeniz, AZ 85040
Lowell E. Foletta
Telephone: (602) 268-2580
Water conditioning and purification systems

Watkins Incorporated
150 Liberty Street, Winona, MN 55987
Richard C. Wantock
Telephone: (507) 457-3300
Household—food, health, and cleaning products

WeCare Distributors, Inc.
200 North Sharon Amity Road, PO Box 222138, Charlotte, NC
    28222
Richard H. Dickens
Telephone: (704) 366-7300
Cosmetics, skin care products

The West Bend Company
400 Washington Street, West Bend, WI 53095
Dale A. Hafeman
Telephone: (414) 334-2311
Cookware, electrical appliances

Winning Edge (The Southwestern Co.)
PO Box 305140, Nashville, TN 37230
George MacIntyre
Telephone: (615) 391-2500
Home safety products—fire alarms and extinguishers, water
    purifiers

World Book, Inc.
510 Merchandise Mart Plaza, Chicago, IL 60654
John E. Frere
Telephone: (312) 245-3456
Educational publications

Yanbal Laboratories
1441 S.W. 33 Place, Ft. Lauderdale, FL 33315
J. Fernando Belmont
Telephone: (305) 524-3200
Cosmetics, skin care products

Zondervan Book of Life
PO Box 6130, Grand Rapids, MI 49506
Robert L. Schmidt
Telephone: (615) 698-3305
Educational publications

Index